Dr Ian Palmer is very well placed to look at the psychological and emotional issues relating to adoption. Adopted himself, he is also a psychiatrist with particular interest in family medicine and psychological trauma. Dr Palmer has wide experience of dealing with individuals and couples attempting to come to terms with difficult experiences and decisions, including going through IVF and contemplating adoption.

WHAT TO EXPECT WHEN YOU'RE ADOPTING . . .

A practical guide to the decisions and emotions
involved in adoption

DR IAN PALMER

Vermilion
LONDON

1 3 5 7 9 10 8 6 4 2

Published in 2009 by Vermilion, an imprint of Ebury Publishing

Ebury Publishing is a Random House Group company

The Random House Group Limited Reg. No. 954009

Addresses for companies within the Random House Group can be found at
www.rbooks.co.uk

A CIP catalogue record for this book is available from the British Library

The Random House Group Limited supports The Forest Stewardship
Council (FSC), the leading international forest certification organisation.
All our titles that are printed on Greenpeace approved FSC certified paper
carry the FSC logo. Our paper procurement policy can be found at
www.rbooks.co.uk/environment

Mixed Sources
Product group from well-managed
forests and other controlled sources
www.fsc.org Cert no. TT-COC-2139
© 1996 Forest Stewardship Council
FSC

Printed and bound in Great Britain by
CPI Mackays, Chatham, ME5 8TD

ISBN 9780091924126

Copies are available at special rates for bulk orders. Contact the sales
development team on 020 7840 8487 for more information.

To buy books by your favourite authors and register for offers, visit
www.rbooks.co.uk

CONTENTS

Acknowledgements

I would like to thank Julia Kellaway, my Commissioning Editor at Vermilion, for having the courage to ask me to write this book and the faith to stay with the project; my wife Triona, for her invaluable advice and support in making this book readable, and my agent Mandy Little, for all her encouragement.

I wish to thank the British Association for Adoption and Fostering (BAAF) for allowing me to reproduce information from their publications and acknowledge both BAAF's and Adoption UK's pre-eminence in this field, and for their continuing crusading work on behalf of children seeking families and parents seeking children.

I wish to thank all the social workers in the field of adoption and fostering for the commitment and hard work they put into ensuring the best possible future for the children in their care, and a special thanks to Lindsay Wright, Team Manager, Islington Adoption Service.

And finally, I want to acknowledge the courage, determination and altruism of adoptive parents for the futures they offer their children. I wish them well in their endeavours and hope that, in some small part, this book will act to swell their numbers.

Any profits from this book will go to Family Futures Charity, a specialist service for children in adoptive families, foster families and families living with children who have experienced separation, loss or early trauma: www.familyfutures.co.uk

Preface

Adoption has always been an integral part of my life, from the very beginning in fact. My story is slightly unusual nowadays as I am a foundling. I was left in a phone box in West London when I was only a few days old. No note, no keepsakes, no name – nothing. Most crucial of all – no clues on how to find my biological mother or father. This fact has been a constant companion throughout my life. My biological mother has never made an attempt to track me down, at least not to my knowledge. I have registered my desire to hear from her with the appropriate agencies, but in more than half a century the silence has been rather loud. I can only assume she is dead, or I am dead to her. I would still love for her to contact me but have absolutely no idea how I would react. Would I be overwhelmed with anger or regress to a needy child? Who knows? I suspect I never will. It doesn't alter the longing though, and I would love to share with her my life story, my successes, my children – her grandchildren.

I would tell her how, while I have achieved much, my life was marred by my adoption. My adoptive mother was a kind but weak soul, whereas my adoptive father was a monster, the stuff of nightmares. He was very abusive, and only later did I learn he had been abused as a child.

My experience was unfortunate but not that uncommon in those days. Such stories are the very reason for many of the changes now in place for adoptive parents and their children. If you add to the mix the fact that my wife gave up a child for adoption when she was very young, you can see that between us we have experienced the 'old' process from both sides of the coin.

I mention these details here because I think it is important for you to understand why I feel driven to write this book. The product of these experiences is knowledge, empathy and a desire to help, even in a small way, to make adoption work for the child and his or her new parents.

I have done well. I have been a GP and subsequently a psychiatrist for more than 30 years, specialising in physical and then psychological trauma and its effect on inter-personal relationships. My professional background gives me the expertise to highlight areas all adoptive parents will have to address at some stage, and to suggest ways to deal with – or better still avoid – the pitfalls that will surely arise as you travel along your adoption journey.

Many of us who have had difficult upbringings want to do our best to make things right for those we love and, at some level, make it 'all right' for ourselves in the process. I am certain my story would have been a different one if I had been adopted by people who had gone through the rigorous procedures that are in place today. In the 1950s, soon after the war, things were very different in Britain. My adoptive parents looked the part – a handsome couple – and were considered ideal in 1953. If they had to go through the same process today, however, not only would my adoptive mother have received help to overcome her emotional difficulties following her stillbirth, but it is likely that my adopted father's character traits would have been noted and set alarm bells ringing. The rigorous assessment programme of today, with its seemingly endless, intrusive questioning, form-filling, interviews and close scrutiny, is there to spot people like him – unsuitable people. Although assessment is now a long and comprehensive process it serves the vital purpose of attempting to ensure the safe and secure match and placement of a disadvantaged child with suitable parents. It is a process with a success rate of 80 per cent or more.

It has not been easy to write this book. This is despite having come to terms in large part with my experience, and even being able to see the positive aspects of it. For example, I am sure I am a much better listener, more empathic and a better doctor because of my adopted father. My journey, like that of all adopted children, is unique. We all have to come to terms with the initial loss or losses in our lives but there is now much greater understanding and help available. There will always be triggers that remind us of our journey – and I wouldn't necessarily recommend writing a book on adoption to someone like me! – but I am a firm believer in seeking solutions. In my view, the best way of dealing with negative experiences is to find the message in them and use this positively as a force for good. I think I am evidence that humans are resilient and can not only survive but even flourish despite a difficult start to life, even a difficult adoption. All children may benefit from adoption. Each child has unique strengths and vulner-abilities, as well as both negative and positive early life experiences.

What is Adoption?

Adoption is when a child (or children) not born to you becomes legally yours. At this point you are equivalent to biological parents in the eyes of the law. You, not their biological parents, have full responsibility for your child or children. Becoming an adoptive parent is one of the most amazing acts any human can undertake. It is for the bold, however quiet, and not the faint-hearted. Given the altruistic nature of the endeavour, the process of adoption may seem unnecessarily long-winded and frustrating, even unfair. You are likely to question why biological parents don't have to go through such a detailed assessment as to their suitability.

Adoption represents one of the most compassionate and humane of all human activities. Individuals open their hearts, their lives, their families and their home to another human being, not born to them, who is in need of security, love and nurturing. The judgement to place a child for adoption is not taken lightly. It is a decision taken in the hope and belief that someone like you will be able to provide a disadvantaged child with a family of their own and the chance of a better future. While an undeniably scary prospect, it is perhaps the greatest gift any human can ever give anyone, including yourself.

Adopting a child will satisfy your desires to parent and, in addition, you will have the satisfaction of knowing that you are special and have been judged by your peers to be good parents. After a series of losses and unsettling change for your child, you will know just how much your child stands to gain through your provision of a home, love and support.

Having children, whether biological or adopted, is a roller coaster of emotions and passions, of highs and lows and of rewards and losses. In most cases the rewards far outweigh the difficulties encountered. These are not simply placatory words to make you feel better; the figures bear out that your chances of getting this right far outweigh the possibility of failure. They show that the vast majority of placements for adoption are successful. This can only mean that the checks and balances in place are effective for both the child and the adoptive parents. I am not suggesting that things are perfect and cannot be improved, but here are a few important facts to keep in the back of your mind for when the going gets tough:

➤ About 95 per cent of applicants succeed in becoming accepted as adoptive parents (those who are turned down can appeal and may be accepted by another agency).
➤ Those accepted will be matched and placed with a child.
➤ Around 80 per cent of all placements are successful.

ADOPTION TODAY

Currently, the average age of a child adopted in the UK is about four years. Taking on a walking, talking little person is quite a different scenario to bringing home a six-week-old bundle who is only just beginning to focus on the world. What we have come to understand is that, whatever the age of your child, it is vitally important to understand as much about them as possible in order to ensure their unique needs are identified and provided for. One of the reasons for a lengthy assessment is to ensure that you are as prepared as you can be to provide a safe and nurturing environment for your children so they are given the opportunity to develop to the maximum of their potential. You will also need help and advice on how to care for yourself so you will be able to keep the show on the road. The task may seem daunting – it is – but don't panic.

There are always solutions and strategies for coping. Nowadays, there is lots of advice and support available for you and your children. Like all parents, at times you will feel isolated, and perhaps it will seem that you are the only parent in the world going through the mangle. Isolation is a dreadful and divisive emotion, often tied up with self-esteem and beliefs about your parenting abilities. Remember, you are not alone. I cannot emphasise this strongly enough: you are not alone. There is more help and advice available now than ever before; you just have to know when to ask for it and where to find it. This book will steer you in the right direction. It will also provide you with a brief guide to dealing with some of the most common difficulties you are likely to encounter.

GOOD TIMING

If you are just beginning the process of adoption your timing is excellent. Responding to the repeated calls for a simplification of the adoption laws and an improvement in the service provided by the agencies involved, the British government undertook a major consultation exercise. This culminated in the 2002 Adoption and Children Act. They didn't rush into this; the Act was a product of reviews that started as long ago as 1992. It eventually came into force in England and Wales in 2005. The main goal of the Act is to encourage more people to adopt, thereby getting children out of the 'care' system and into a secure, safe and nurturing family environment. The Adoption and Children (Scotland) Act of 2007 is due to come into force in 2009. Northern Ireland takes its lead in developing legislation in this area from England and Wales.

The government listened to experts, including adoptive parents and adopted children. Their deliberations examined parenting in its widest context and the many and varied ways that humans care for, love and nurture children. This endeavour paved the way for a greater understanding of diversity in parenting. In turn, this opened the door to considering a much greater pool of people as suitable to become adoptive parents, including those who are single, civil partners, people who are unmarried and same-sex couples.

The idea was to untangle the legal spaghetti that created lengthy delays and put a lot of people off contemplating adoption. The Act also aimed to improve the performance of adoption services, particularly in the long-term advice and support offered to adopting families once a placement had been made. This more 'user friendly' approach by the powers that be had a lot to do with the fact that the number of adoptions had fallen in England and Wales.

The Office of National Statistics keeps records on trends in adoption practice.[1,2] In 1971 there were 21,495 Adoption Orders (Adoptions) in England and Wales. In 2002, this had fallen to 5,680, and by 2006, 4,764. In the year up to 31 March 2007, 2,735 children were placed for adoption in England and Wales. Between 1996 and 2006 there were increases in the proportion of children adopted between the ages of one to four and a reduction in the five to fourteen age group. The rapid decline in the number of children available for adoption followed the introduction of legal abortion in 1967 and the implementation of the Children Act 1975, which allowed magistrates to award custody of a child or children to an adult, be they one of the parents or another family member, in order that the child might receive the care and attention they required. In the year ending 31 March 2007 there were 64,640 children looked after by local authorities in England and Wales, with slightly more boys than girls (56 to 44 per cent).

HOW TO USE THIS BOOK

The aim of this book is to encourage you to offer yourselves as adoptive parents by giving you an insight into the process. If you know what to expect you will have a much better chance of managing the many and various challenges that will come your way when you adopt a child. Please note that, unless otherwise indicated, this book focuses on practice in England and Wales.

Remember, seeking permanent solutions for 'looked-after' children is currently high up the political and social agenda. There is a renewed interest in the issue, perhaps because the numbers of children being placed is continuing to drop despite the fact that the number of children needing a family is growing. If you were cynical you would conclude that this renewed interest in adoption had more than a little to do with the high cost to the authorities of bringing thousands of children up in foster and care homes. A more generous mind would see the moves to make the process more accessible as altruistic and child-friendly – how else are children to be offered the benefits of a 'normal' family life? As potential adopting parents it actually doesn't matter which view applies; what is important is getting it right for everyone involved. If things are more in your favour these days it is the result of the new legislation, and that is all to the good.

The sheer number of publications about adoption can be bewildering and somewhat overwhelming. Where do you start? Well, clearly if you are reading this, you have chosen this book as one of your guides, and I hope it will prove to be a good choice for you. I have tried to make it possible for you to get the information you need in one publication rather than having to buy everything you find on the bookshelf or scour the internet. With that in mind I have read many thousands of words on this subject by, amongst others, adoption experts, adoptive parents, adopted children and journalists, and tried to bring together what I see as the most useful kernels of information. There is a full bibliography at the end of this book so you can explore further areas that are of particular interest to you at your leisure.

This book starts with a look at the issues you will need to face when you begin to consider adoption. Part Two explains the mechanics of the adoption process, including the assessment, taking into account the currently changing picture due to the new Adoption and Children Act. As a psychiatrist, the legal aspects of adoption are not my area of expertise but I will touch upon them as it is important for you to have at least a rudimentary understanding.

Throughout the book I will focus on the emotional and personal experience of adoption, both before and after a placement is made. Communication is a theme throughout – communication between you, your child, the adoption agency, your family and the professionals. Other areas explored include normal childhood development; how children develop attachment behaviours; and how you develop emotional bonds with your child. We'll look at what can go wrong, and how to deal with it. I will also explore context, which is another important issue when trying to understand your child.

Remember, you are unique, your child is unique and each placement is different. Everyone brings their own distinctive perspective to the journey. This book aims to provide you with details of what to expect and how to negotiate the twists and turns in your journey to parenthood. I hope it will encourage you to seek advice from professionals should the need arise and not 'suffer in silence', which will benefit neither you nor your child.

The best way of pursuing this difficult but rewarding path to adopting a child is to arm yourself with as much knowledge as your head can cope with. If you know what you are doing and what to expect, and have an idea of how to handle it, then you stand an excellent chance of getting this right. Acquiring this information is an investment for the future, both for you and for the child who finds a home with you.

THE TIMESCALE FOR ADOPTION

As you might expect there is a pathway and a timescale to the legal process of adoption. This culminates in the granting of an Adoption Order by a court, at which point you are the legal parent of your child and have full parental rights. This book aims to take you through this process a step at a time. Contemplation is the first step. Depending on how you come to adoption, there can be no time put on how long it takes you to move from an initial, perhaps fleeting, thought to actually contacting an adoption agency. You may have discussed your thoughts with your friends, family or partner; you may have read books such as this or trawled the internet. When you are ready, you start the journey by contacting an adoption agency.

You may attend an adoption and fostering 'event' run locally where you can talk directly to agency staff, foster and adoptive parents and learn more about adoption and fostering. You will be welcomed and able to get clear advice from experts, be they social workers or parents, and information to take away and read. A member of the team may contact you later to see if you want to proceed. If you ring the agency they should provide you with written information within five working days. They will probably talk to you briefly on the phone about the pros and cons of adoption and then, if you want to proceed, arrange an informal meeting, either in your home or at their office, to discuss your situation and desires. This should happen within six to eight weeks of your initial expression of interest.

If you decide to continue you will formally apply in writing and the agency will decide whether to take you on. If they do not, do not despair; another agency may be more than happy to do so. If they decline your application they must do you the courtesy of explaining their decision. Once you have been accepted the whole process from this date to the agency recommendation as to your suitability should take no longer than eight months. This cannot be written in stone as each case is different, and must be dealt with individually. Some assessments will be shorter, some longer. Your social worker should keep you aware of the timescale and explain any deviations.

Once you have been accepted there then follows the exciting part: the search for your child. This may have commenced during your assessment; for example, your social worker (or you) may have a particular child in mind. The matter of supply and demand comes into play here. The adoption agency will inform you which age groups, types and numbers of children you will be considered for. It then becomes a search for a match. You may have to wait weeks or months but seldom more than a year; it all depends on finding a suitable match. Although frustrating at times it is important to remember how important this process is to your child. No corners should be cut. It is too important a decision to rush.

Once a match has been found and formally agreed by the adoption panel, a Placement Order is issued. This is followed by introductions and meetings. The time involved will vary according to the age of the child, and is much quicker with infants. Once the decision is made, however, it is important not to delay things too long. If all goes well, your child should be placed with you within about six weeks. Once your child is with you the agency will arrange a review of how things are going at four weeks and then every three months until the Adoption Order is granted. If your child is placed with you by an adoption agency you can apply to the courts for an Adoption Order after the child has been with you for 10 weeks.

It therefore takes about eight to 10 months from initial contact with the agency to being accepted as an adoptive parent; up to a similar period (usually much less) waiting for a match; up to six weeks until your child enters your family; 10 weeks until you can apply for an Adoption Order, after which it will depend on the legal processes involved. It is perhaps best to expect that the whole process is likely to take about two years from start to finish. If you choose to adopt from abroad the timescale is likely to be longer (see Chapter 2, page 60).

Once you have decided to start the ball rolling you will be treading a well-worn path. You will be swept up by the momentum and the requirements of the process and the novelty of the experience. It will be a heady mix of excitement and discovery – not only about your child but also about yourself.

Good luck.

PART ONE:

CONSIDERING ADOPTION

CHAPTER 1

Is Adoption for You?

It is highly likely that you are reading this after months, perhaps years, of thinking about having a child. The idea will not be a new one, so you have already invested a lot of emotional energy into the subject. Adoption may have been your first or only choice; you may have had to come to terms with your infertility. Whatever the background, what you are planning to do is admirable and courageous. Your actions will bring a lifetime of joy not just to you, but to a child whose early prospects were bleak. Having said that, you have to be 100 per cent certain that this is the right course of action for you, and those close to you. Dig deep, search your head and heart before committing to adoption; the consequences of getting it wrong are potentially devastating to all involved. It is not a simple question to resolve, so this chapter is designed to help you make your decision by identifying the questions you need to ask and helping you to answer them.

CHANGING ATTITUDES

Like the type and number of children available for adoption today, the make-up of adoptive parents has changed considerably in the past few decades. The assessment process has had to move with the times to accommodate the different way society sees the 'family'. We are much more inclusive these days. Twenty-five years ago, social workers would have sought an 'ideal' couple. This stereotype would have been drawn from cultural norms including marriage, heterosexuality and moral standing (presumably deduced from the applicants' position in society, profession or job and attendance at church). This stereotype represented stability, and like today, getting the child into a strong, stable home was of the utmost importance. Unlike today, placing a child with single parents or gay and lesbian couples would have been un-heard of. Indeed, the suggestion alone would have caused outrage. Today we are much more open about these issues and take a broader view. The emphasis has moved away from an individual's sexual orientation or marital status. Now the agencies are looking at the quality of the potential parenting.

As children's needs have changed, local authorities have tried to broaden their search for adoptive parents who more closely represent the ethnic, cultural and religious diversity of some of these disadvantaged children. Our con-temporary understanding of psychological security has also moved on. Adoption agencies now look for evidence of competence in potential adopters. To do this, the assess-ment examines what things you have achieved and how you have achieved them, overcome obstacles and managed change across your life. You should find this a learning and empowering experience, and it should also provide realistic and in-depth information for your social worker.

Our knowledge of child and human development, and the importance of the early formative years, has become much more sophisticated. This has also influenced thinking about care and adoption. Changes to the assessment process have been driven by an increased understanding of the processes of attachment, bonding, loss and change across the life cycle. The old psychoanalytical theories have been augmented by behavioural and neuro-cognitive theories. Knowledge of how real-world and real-life experiences impact on a child is growing, and with it an understanding of what different parents can bring to adoption.

WHO CAN ADOPT?

A more pertinent question might be 'who cannot adopt?' As the law stands, there is nothing to stop most people applying and having a good chance of succeeding. Legally, people cannot be denied the right to be considered as an adoptive parent on grounds of race, sexuality, background or marital status. Gay and lesbian couples, single parents and people from different ethnic groups have just as much right to adopt as the traditional stereotype of the respectable married couple.

There are, however, some restrictions:

➤ You must be over 21, unless you are the birth parent in a joint step-parent adoption, in which case you must be 18 or over. The average age of adopters in the UK is 38.

➤ There is no upper age limit, although common sense will come into play and most agencies would like there to be less than a 45-year age difference between you and your adopted child.

➤ You will not be considered if you have been convicted or cautioned for any offences against children. This applies to anyone over 18 in your household.

➤ You may be excluded if you have been convicted of certain sexual offences against adults.

➤ You may be able to adopt if you have certain other criminal offences but these will have to be taken on a case-by-case basis. Remember, they are likely to be revealed through the criminal records check and so you must be honest with your adoption agency from the outset if this is not to count against you.

➤ You must be domiciled in the UK (i.e. your permanent home is in the UK) or 'habitually resident' in the UK for at least 12 months. Habitual residence relates to issues such as the duration, continuity, family ties and stability of your residence in the UK. If you are in any doubt about this seek legal advice early on.

➤ You cannot become an adoptive parent unless you have been assessed and approved by a recognised adoption agency in the UK; it is not possible to arrange an adoption with a birth parent or family without going through due legal process.

There are other exclusions that do not fit neatly into bullet points. This is because they may be temporary or relate to local custom and practice. The list of potential issues that may interfere with adoption is quite long. It may seem intrusive when these issues are examined but it is essential. Remember, everyone wants the same thing: a safe placement of a child.

HONESTY IS THE BEST POLICY

It is important to tell the adoption agency about anything currently happening in your life that may interfere with the adoption or assessment or complicate or compromise the relationship you will need to form with your adoptive child if the adoption is to succeed. For instance, you should tell them about any ongoing fertility treatment. You may not be accepted by an agency for assessment until this is finished because it is important to have come to some 'closure'. In other words, you need to have been able to grieve for what cannot be and to be ready to invest all your commitment and energies in giving your adopted child the best you can.

You should also be honest about any relationship problems you may be having. Relationships are at the root of making a family and providing safety and security for your child. Your current relationships must therefore be in good repair. Trying to cover the cracks may be okay if it is just you two, but the stresses of the assessment and the addition of a child – your child – will seldom improve the situation. It could be disastrous not only to you but also your child if your relationship fails later and you had not addressed the problems before you adopted your child. Remember, it is all about giving your child the best chance.

The assessment process offers you the time, space and support to examine your motives, and many individuals and couples come to see this as valuable in its own right, a chance to re-examine and re-evaluate where they are emotionally.

CHILDREN SEEKING ADOPTION

In 2006 just over 4,700 Adoption Orders were passed in the courts of England and Wales,[3] and these children became the legal responsibility of their adoptive parents. These children are the central characters in the drama of adoption.

They come in all shapes and sizes. Any child under the age of 18 can be adopted, although the majority of adoptions involve children aged one to four. Older children are more difficult to place for adoption for a number of reasons, not least because of their wishes, and they are more likely to receive a Special Guardianship Order (see page 68). It is estimated that there are currently about 4,000 children waiting to be adopted in the UK.[4] They range from infants through to young adolescents and come from a wide variety of backgrounds.

Some come from an environment where the mother or father, or both, simply cannot cope, despite their best efforts and support. Children come from all ethnic groups. Some may have physical or learning difficulties, they may be disabled or have chronic ongoing medical or psychological conditions. Many are likely to have had a troubled background but this is not inevitable, although loss and separation are common to all. Every child is different and has his or her own particular needs. As a general rule, adoptive parents who can offer a family to sibling groups are welcomed. This is a daunting prospect for many but does ensure that small family groups stay together, where appropriate.

All children will have spent some time in care, usually with foster parents. Ideally, they will not have moved too frequently but stability is not always possible. There may, for example, have been a number of failed attempts to return the child to their close or extended biological family. Each placement, separation and loss has a huge emotional impact on children. Such moves are like small bereavements which must be acknowledged and, where appropriate, examined and worked through at some level. This will ensure that the child realises and accepts that adoption is a secure placement 'forever'.

THE FIRST STEP – CONTEMPLATING ADOPTION

The idea of adopting a child is not something that will have just popped into your head. It is unlikely you will have had a 'light bulb moment'. Generally, the process of contemplating this huge step will have taken time, and developed its own momentum. There are stages of contemplation. Your initial consideration will have been to see adoption as a possible course of action. That will have prompted a deeper study of the subject. You will have talked it through with your partner, family and friends, and possibly with work colleagues and your doctor. You will have studied the subject at length, reflecting, deliberating and meditating before taking that daunting first step.

During this period of contemplation you are likely to have developed your own expectations about adoption and what tomorrow holds. Expectations are the images we create in our mind, the hopes or beliefs we hold that something will happen. They are not to be dismissed as they are about the future, and without them we probably wouldn't get started on many projects. Imagination, when based on everyday realities, is a key driver in creating achievable expectations. Imagination based on fantasy, on the other hand, creates 'great expectations' which are unlikely to be achievable. Having realistic expectations is a tricky call. It requires the enthusiasm of an optimist tempered with the pragmatism of the pessimist – the optimistic pessimist!

The first move is in your hands – you are the one who sets the whole process in motion by seeking out the adoption agency. You are firmly in the driving seat at that point. It will be your choice to talk to agency workers, go to educational events and meet other people in your situation. The next bit – making a formal application – is also down to you. Once that is received, however, the adoption machine is fired up and the agency/authority swings into action. Essentially, they are in control of the next part of the process. They will decide whether or not to take you on; they run the assessment and decide if you are suitable for adoption. Other fixed points that are out of your control are the decision of the adoption panel to approve you, and finally the granting of the Adoption Order which makes you the legal parent of your child.

This will be an emotional roller coaster for you, and even more so for your child. To safeguard all of you the law is a constant companion throughout this process. The Adoption and Children Act 2002 makes the welfare of the child of paramount importance for adoption agencies in their deliberations and decisions. The courts are involved in your child's journey to adoption from the outset. For example, if a local authority believes your child should be put up for adoption against the wishes of the biological parents, they are required to apply for a Placement Order. Legislation exists in order to protect not just your child but everyone involved. For most of us the idea of getting involved in any legal matters is daunting, but you will find that if all is going to plan the law will be sitting quietly in the shadows, only moving to centre stage if necessary.

The first time you are likely to come across the courts is when an Adoption Order is made – the final hurdle. Both you and your child will attend this hearing. This legal stage is the culmination of months, probably years, of hard work. It is when, in the eyes of the law, you become responsible for your child. You are the new parent. Once you have that piece of paper clutched in one hand and the child in the other the moment will have come to crack open the champagne, an occasion to savour and cherish. After what you have all been through it's right to take time to celebrate before getting on with the business of being a family.

WHY DO YOU WANT TO ADOPT?

There are myriad reasons why people wish to adopt. Whatever the reason, there is one overarching powerful desire and that is to be a parent – whether it's for the first time or again, and even again.

INFERTILITY

Most of us assume we are fertile. We expend a lot of time and energy in our youth trying to avoid pregnancy at all costs. The message we get from our families and society is to hang on until the time is right, whatever that means. How ironic then that some of us reach the stage in our lives when we want children and discover to our amazement that it is not possible. Certainly it's irritating but the realisation that something is wrong cuts much deeper than mere annoyance. The drive to reproduce is biological and cultural. It is ingrained into the fabric of our minds, lives and beings. The accepted 'default' position is fertility, and this is tied into issues of potency for males, fecundity for women, parenting, nurturing, continuing the family line, leaving something behind and so on.

The pressures to conceive are huge and they come from a number of directions. First and foremost, they come from within, hardwired into us by dear old Mother Nature. There is no escaping the internal clock that ticks away like a time bomb. At the end of the day we are just mammals, and the urge or need to procreate is as basic as the requirement to eat and sleep. Once the hormones kick in it is difficult to switch them off. They gnaw away, creating a void that can be filled only with a child.

Then there are the considerable external pressures. Take a look around you. See how often you are confronted with images that involve family life. The message is everywhere and overpowering. Pick up a newspaper and you see it in stories and adverts; watch the television and the family features prominently. You find the same in literature and films. In fact, you would be hard-pressed to escape from the message that parenting is advisable, if not essential. Children are the future and therefore our culture demands that we all do our bit. Learning that you cannot deliver this requirement in the face of such compulsion comes as a blow. Sometimes people who cannot have children feel stigmatised.

Infertility can be primary, secondary or voluntary. Primary infertility is either known about from the outset of a relationship or found out after fruitless attempts to conceive. Secondary infertility happens after couples have already had a child and have failed to go on to conceive another. Voluntary infertility is where you choose not to have a baby through conception. Choosing not to have children, as opposed to having this choice removed from you through infertility, remains an unusual decision, and one that is not well understood. These individuals may be seen as abnormal and as not pulling their weight, even when they decide to adopt children rather than bear them. There are many reasons for voluntary infertility, and individuals or couples choosing not to conceive together but to adopt must expect to explain their motivations.

The significance of infertility for you and your family is recognised by adoption agencies and will be examined in depth during your assessment. Accepting infertility involves a process of grief and mourning. Your adoption agency will want to know where you are in this process as it is important that you have grieved properly. Social workers are trained to understand how people cope with grief and loss, so expect – indeed demand – that your infertility is dealt with in a sensitive and constructive manner.

Ideally before, but certainly during, the assessment it will be important to know that you are settled in your own mind and have accepted you will be unable to have children. You will need to be comfortable with the changes this will have created in relation to your self-image – as well as issues relating to masculinity and femininity, potency and impotency – and be at peace with their social implications.

If you have been trying to have a baby through IVF you will have had years of living with the fear that you cannot get pregnant. It is a painful process that is likely to have left its mark on you. It will be particularly important to have come through the frequently unpleasant or even traumatic experience that IVF can be and the difficulties it can create in your relationship. For many it is frequently a great relief to be able to step away from a medical intervention that can have unpleasant side-effects on your relationship. These can include damage to love and intimacy by removing the passion of conception and replacing it with a cold and clinical scientific process.

You and your social worker should be able to accept that the past is firmly in the past, while acknowledging the importance of the loss, and you are now ready to invest fully in adoption.

ALTRUISM

People who choose to adopt when they could have a child naturally are usually motivated by altruism. They wish to share what they have with someone many times less fortunate, to give hope to the hopeless. Going down this route is a praiseworthy act indeed, and one that makes so much difference to another living soul. In the world of adoption, families who choose to adopt in this way are particularly prized, especially as they often have children of their own already. This means they can offer parenting experience from the 'coalface', and the adopted child will be going to a home that is tried and tested. They will have a ready-made family group, with all the pros and cons of being the new face in the house. This scenario can and does work well.

HOW YOU GOT TO THIS POINT

Part of preparing to adopt involves getting to know your-self better. In particular, you need to attempt to understand what has motivated you. There are plenty of reasons to take this path but each of us has our own story to tell. You have come to adoption from your unique background. It is important to get a feel for what that is and how it has affected you. The clearer you are about how you got to this point, the better able you will be to stand by your decision.

A useful exercise is to consider the following. Most of us grow up with a knowledge of fertility. We learn about infertility as we get older and have a better understanding of reproduction. But at what point did you learn about adoption? How did the concept come into your life? It may have been in a positive way. Equally, it may have been something traumatic. Perhaps you know people who were adopted, or who have adopted. They may be members of your wider family. Think about their experiences and consider how it might have coloured your views on adoption. For some people events in the news can be a powerful influence. Seeing orphans tied into their cots in Romania lying in their own faeces will trigger a wish to do something for helpless children. If your experience of adoption has been negative, turn your thoughts within and examine whether you have come to terms with that. Have you made your peace with the past? Can you look forward to the future in a positive way?

I don't mean to shake your resolve but you must remember that adoption is a permanent step which must be entered into with 100 per cent commitment. There is no room for doubt. It is just like having a child naturally – there may be occasions when part of you wants to hand them back but you can't; they are yours to care for through thick and thin. The bad times will be outweighed by the good. In life you have both ends of the spectrum, and it is the balance that contributes to what we regard as normality. While there may be plenty of people within your support network to help if needs be, this is not true for all adopting parents; but quality can always outweigh quantity. It is important to recognise the importance of supportive social networks, however small, in making your adoption a success.

What you bring to this equation is your whole self – not just the clever bit that can get to grips with the ins and outs of the adoption process but also the bit deep inside that makes you what you are. Some would call it a soul, others simply your personality. Whatever name you give it, you are going to need to be able to commit that self to your child.

Although knowledge is vitally important in making life-changing decisions such as adoption, you will – indeed must – listen to your heart. Hard facts are all very well but they are not enough. This life change goes beyond anything else you are likely to have done. It involves all aspects of you as an individual. The reality is that you have to throw everything at it, your emotions, passions and resiliencies. Those ingredients make you who you are and are vital to the success of adopting a child. So, too, are the human values that will see you through the periodic difficulties you are likely to encounter with your child in the years to come.

Some of you will have made the decision to adopt from a starting point of joy; others from terrible sadness and loss. All this is relevant to how you move ahead with adoption. These factors are part of your make-up, integral to who you are and therefore of great relevance to the child you bring into your life. If there are problems within then sort them out now. You will definitely benefit, and so will your new family member.

Now is a good moment to learn how not to put off that bit of 'me time', to give yourself permission to indulge in what might appear to be a luxury but is in fact an essential part of making this venture work. It is important to be able to take a bit of space for yourself. You may already have mastered this art, but in this busy world taking time out is often the bit we push to the backburner. As you go through the adoption process, carve out a niche where you can pause, reflect and take stock. Like all long trips – and this one is for life – you must look after yourself in order to get through it in one piece. After all, how can you offer the best to someone else if you don't first have that same consideration for yourself?

MAKING DECISIONS

We are all good at making decisions, although most of us take this talent for granted as it is an habitual way of dealing with the world. From the moment we hop out of bed in the morning we are masters of decision-making. Will it be coffee or tea? Sugar or sweeteners? Skimmed or semi-skimmed milk? We become aware of our ability to make decisions only when we stop to think about it, or when we lose this ability, such as when we are depressed.

When confronted with life-changing choices, you become aware of how you make decisions. Most of us contemplate making a decision only if we 'have to', and can generally think of a zillion reasons for delaying this fateful moment. However, after all your wishful thinking, avoidance behaviours, rationalisations and the like, you will eventually feel impelled to edge towards making a decision – if not actually grabbing the bull by the horns.

Making the conscious decision to adopt will focus your mind. It will give you the drive to move forwards and concentrate on the process to come. Any ambivalence should be banished as you seek to answer the question: 'Is adoption for me?' You can answer this question only by throwing yourself into the process of obtaining information, and meeting and talking to people who can provide you with the necessary impetus and incentive to move on. You will gain a healthy and realistic understanding of the challenges ahead and how you will deal with them.

Having said that, adoption is not something you should rush into. When you make that decision you have to mean it. For the sake of all involved you should be as certain as you can that this is the way you want to go. You are the one driving this. If you are in doubt it is perfectly okay to stop the process, wait for time to pass and re-examine your options at a later date. It is important that you have as much realistic information as you can and there is no shame in delaying your decision.

There are lots of theories about how to make decisions. While we know that a dispassionate eye is highly desirable, most of us have to accept that our emotional and irrational side will get in the way at times. You're only human after all, so be easy on yourself. For most of us, decisions about parenting and nurturing can never be wholly and clinically devoid of emotions – thank heavens. Your determination, resilience and passion to parent will guide your decisions and desire to become an adoptive parent.

ADOPTION IS AN IRREVERSIBLE STEP

If you are in any way uncomfortable about the total commitment required for adoption then it is not for you. You will need to be aware that your motives and motivations for adoption will be discussed and explored in detail. It is important therefore that you are clear about why you are contemplating becoming adoptive parents at this time.

Once an Adoption Order is signed you are legally responsible for the child. He or she becomes your child. You are as responsible as a birth parent and remain so forever. Your social worker and local authority will want to reassure themselves and the adoption panel that you are making an informed decision, and it is their job to provide you with the information you need to make it.

DECIDING NOT TO ADOPT

At any stage of the process you may decide that adoption is not for you and that you would prefer to live your life without children. Most individuals or couples who make this decision do so as a result of life events and issues related to quality of life and their relationship. Other influences can include world poverty and overcrowding. One of the main reasons for the long assessment period before adoption is to help you make the right decision for you.

Some people who have endured unsuccessful fertility treatment find the prospect of the adoption process too much to contemplate. When all things are balanced, life free of children may be equally rewarding. Being child-free does not necessarily mean children are not in your life. There are numerous ways of interacting with children, ranging from those in your close or extended family through involvement in youth work, children's charities to perhaps even sponsoring children abroad. Whatever your input, you can make changes.

There are many ways of living a good and fulfilling life without either adopting or bearing children. All lives have value and every decision has its consequences, both positive and negative. The decision to live your life free of children is not an easy one to make and is seldom helped by insensitivity within society. Whatever your decision, it is important to seek help and advice from those you love and trust, and perhaps even professionals. The decision should be positive as this will help you to 'move on' in your life to a more fulfilling place and not dwell on the past.

SEEKING ADVICE AND INFORMATION

There is a huge amount of information out there on the subject of adoption, possibly more than anyone could read! You will be keen to get more information but it is important not to become overwhelmed and possibly confused.

THE INTERNET

The internet is a wonderful resource. The BBC website on adoption is particularly good. It provides a mine of useful information presented in an accessible way, as well as links to the various agencies and resources involved in adoption in the UK. Perhaps most important of all, it can be trusted as being accurate. The problem with the internet is that many sites are not audited in any way, so the information you come across may not be correct. It is important to be cautious and selective about what you read and where your information comes from. In the Resources section (page 248) I have listed the addresses of websites that I feel are useful and generally considered trustworthy.

THE LIBRARY

The library is a useful source of printed information. It will have books on adoption in stock, or enable you to order some of the huge number of publications available. Libraries are also excellent information centres for local authority services such as adoption. These are frequently advertised in the library, or your librarian will be able to advise you on how to find out more. Perhaps one of the most useful sources of printed material is the British Association for Adoption and Fostering (BAAF). I would thoroughly recommend their publications and website to you. Details of useful books are included in the Resources section (page 250).

OTHER PEOPLE

You may be surprised by the number of your friends and family who either know someone, or know of someone, who has adopted or been adopted. It is worth asking around. Once you mention that you are interested in adoption, people tend to immediately relate their own knowledge of the subject. The world of adoption is bigger than you think, so chances are you won't have to rely on books or the internet to come across people with first-hand experience. They are probably right under your nose. If, however, you are 'just thinking' about the whole issue, that's fine. Before discussing it with other people, you need to explore, reflect on and clarify your emotional reactions.

ADOPTION AGENCIES

The best way of getting your hands on the facts is to go to the horse's mouth – the people who run adoption services in your area. They are geared up for this type of contact; for them your enquiry is precious. Without you they would not be able to function. In conjunction with your other enquiries, contact your local authority adoption agency or a voluntary agency directly. You will find their contact details on the internet or in the phone book (see also the Resources section, page 248, for national organisations that will help, particularly BAAF).

Agencies will provide you with up-to-date, honest and clear information. I cannot recommend this route more highly. You are likely to find a warm reception and plenty of information, and you will be able to have an honest dialogue with committed personnel. The agencies involved know that it will have taken a lot of courage for you to embrace adoption as the way forward. If your experience is less than positive from the moment you contact one of them, and you do not feel welcomed, listened to or taken seriously, try another agency. Remember, at this point you have not committed yourself to any course of action with any specific agency. You are still seeking information and advice. You are in the driving seat and can shop around for the agency or authority that suits you best.

STUDY GROUPS

Study groups are frequently offered before and/or during the assessment process. They are a fantastic way of getting information. All authorities and agencies offer a range of guidance for adoptive parents. They differ from area to area, and your social worker will explain what is on offer. You will probably be given an outline when you go to the first adoption meeting or during your first phone call.

Some adoption agencies run preparation meetings and groups over a number of weeks in the evenings or at weekends. A number will try and squeeze the whole process into two or three whole days. Many potential adoptive parents find the short sharp events preferable to the more drawn-out ones but, however they are organised, the information and experience remain the same. Some agencies require you to attend these study days and groups before they will accept your application. Others, however, will crack on with your assessment and the education groups will run concurrently. It's a bit of a lottery. If this concerns you then ask about it when you make your first enquiries, and get a rundown of how the agency deals with applications. If you aren't happy try another one that may work more to your liking.

Although you might not be keen to mix with others going through this process it is advisable to give it a go. No one will force you along to meetings but your ability to integrate is regarded as important. The gatherings or study periods are usually group activities. If you have a partner they should attend the meetings with you; not to do so would give an unclear message about your or your partner's commitment to adoption.

Any gathering of complete strangers can provoke anxiety. Your group leader should be aware of this and be able to spot anyone having difficulties. These meetings are educational, not therapeutic. There will, however, be some therapeutic elements, such as the sharing of particular experiences. Some of the topics discussed may resonate with an earlier, and possibly unpleasant, life event. For example, your reactions to the issues thrown up by children being taken into care and looked after will be explored. You might be surprised how this exercise can actually be quite positive and empowering. You will hear about separation and loss in these children, and this may remind you of similar bereavements in your own life. You don't have to stand up and discuss any of this with the rest of the people there. Then again, if you do feel that a sensitive button has been pressed and there is something you need to get off your chest, tell the group leader or your social worker. It might have kicked up issues that you would benefit from talking about. Issues of separation and loss are very important to consider as you will need to help your child accept their past so that they can move on in their life. This holds true for adults as well.

In these study groups you will be introduced to harrowing cases of children who have been subject to neglect, inconsistent parenting and physical or sexual abuse. It is vitally important you are fully aware of the realities of your child's past. Knowledge is power. Secrets can only fester and compound problems if not acknowledged and addressed. Only when problems are identified can solutions be found. Although you may have read of these horrors in the media, hearing about them in graphic detail can be distressing. So be prepared to hear some disturbing tales and remember you can make a difference. Group sessions are designed in such a way that the experience of hearing such details can help defuse some of the tension and dissipate any acute distress you may feel. After all, you are there to help children avoid or escape from a loveless existence. How often do we look at others less fortunate than ourselves and wish we could do something more than pop a few coins in a collection tin? Well, no one can do more than give another human being the chance of a good and loving family. You are likely to leave the meeting with much to think about.

Most of us have had the experience of feeling uncomfortable in group situations, if only from our time at school. Before the group leader arrives, you may find it easy to chat freely with other group members, but when it all goes quiet, the whole feeling of the event changes. This is perfectly normal and your leader should be adept at 'warming you up' and dissipating this tension. It is worth remembering that you don't have to ask questions to learn a lot in a group. Others may ask the questions you would like to have asked and you can benefit from the answers. Group leaders will be familiar with the sort of questions that come up and will be able to fill in any awkward spaces.

The study periods encourage you to contemplate not only your journey in adoption. You will also be thinking about the children for whom adoption is considered to be in their best interests. You will cover topics related to child development and attachment but also ethnic, religious and other cultural issues. In this area there are a multitude of right answers. Sometimes it is not the answers that matter so much as your way of thinking about issues, such as how flexible you are in your way of thinking, and how rigidly you hold to your beliefs. Flexibility and tolerance are sought. You will be asked for your take on matters of faith and religion, how they influence your life and how they will affect any child placed with you. Attempts will be made to ensure your children share your ethnic background, religious beliefs and practices, wherever possible.

HOW ADOPTION AFFECTS OTHER PEOPLE IN YOUR LIFE

It is essential to consider how adoption will affect the important people in your life. You will be unable to move forwards towards your goal of adoption unless you all work together. Remember that during your assessment the social worker will speak to your partner, children and other important people in your life about your application for adoption; not talking to them is not an option. You are all in this together and that is how you will be viewed by the agency.

YOUR PARTNER

Although adoption has been opened up to single parents and same-sex couples, it is still predominantly something undertaken by two people, usually a man and a woman. While your family and friends are important, the person you start and end each day with is vital. Their role is key to the success of the adoption process. The decision to adopt has to come from both of you. After all, you are a team, and taking on a new member of the family is a huge choice to make. You will have equal shares in the responsibilities ahead.

The child will change your lives and your relationship forever, just as the arrival of a naturally conceived baby would. When I speak of 'change' I do not mean something negative. We all want to cling on to certainties, keep things as they are, but if you take time to think this through you will notice that change is happening all the time. It is absolutely normal. You will already be used to how life evolves; you may just never have had the occasion to sit down and notice it.

You will have shared the early part of this journey, from the realisation that you want to adopt to making tentative initial enquiries. The process is likely to bring you closer. You may have had years of trying for a baby, and that will have put enormous pressure on you both, but you have come through it. You are still together and planning for the future. As they say, what doesn't kill you makes you stronger. You can see adoption as a gift, giving you the child you would never otherwise have had.

Then again, if you are in a relationship and your other half is not aware of your views and plans in this respect then you need to take a serious look at what is going on between the two of you. Something isn't quite right and it should be sorted out before you go ahead with involving an adopted child in your domestic problems. Is one of you pushing for this while the other is uncertain or even against it? If you don't deal with these problems now they will come back to haunt you later, and by then you will have committed to your new family. Rocky foundations are risky. It will pay massive dividends to pause the process and sort things out with your partner at this stage. Once you are both happy with the plan then you can move ahead and be a force to be reckoned with. You will also be much happier and therefore better parents.

Your relationship should provide you both with support and encouragement at all stages of the adoption process. Agencies will want to be reassured, as far as possible, that you are a solid couple, and they will look to the past and present for evidence that this is so. It may be that you have never had any worries about how you two get on. You could be the proverbial peas in a pod – made for each other. Then again, you are likely to have had your run-ins over the years. Everyone does and it's a completely normal dynamic. If you have been together for a long time your relationship will have grown and evolved through the ups and downs that life dishes out. Being in a couple is not a static position – the roller coaster is part of the package.

It is therefore of fundamental importance that you enter the adoption process with a good feeling about your partnership. Life experiences should have led to personal growth and intimacy between the two of you. As you take steps towards having a child you would be well advised to reappraise how you get on, and have a clear view about how you see the years ahead and a commitment to that shared future. Although starting a family is scary, the prospect should feel exciting, exhilarating and challenging all at once. These are powerful positive emotions so enjoy them.

When you live with someone, once the initial honeymoon period wears off you get on with the business of living. This involves falling into habitual ways of being. Consider how you run your lives now. For example, how do you apportion roles and responsibilities in the household? How do you resolve disputes? What keeps you together? What are your shared ambitions, goals and targets? You can expect to cover this ground with your social worker. Part of this will be an examination of your relationship and its stability. This also gives you an opportunity to consider the things you might have to change when your child comes into your home. There will be times when such questioning seems intrusive. It will help to remember that your social worker is only trying to discharge their legal responsibilities and ensure that a child placed with you is safe and secure. You may not want to hang out your dirty laundry but, oddly enough, doing so will help all those involved.

YOUR CHILDREN

If you already have children you will have considered their views or talked to them about the possibility of having a new family member, depending on their age and under-standing. Children may bring up the subject of another brother or sister – they may even prompt your contemplation. Many people feel that it is best for children to have siblings, but who knows what's right? If both you and your child or children are 'up for it' from the start they may be as excited as you! If, on the other hand, it is only the grown-ups who are thinking about extending the family, you are in the same situation as biological parents who may or may not talk to their other children about having another child. It may just be sprung upon them! You will know your child's temperament and should be able to gauge how best to break the news. Clearly you will have thought about the ramifications before you present your child or children with the news – but if you have decided, that is it. If you are excited, they are likely to be excited. Remember, children pick up all your non-verbal cues (body language, tone of voice and the like), and if you're unsure they'll notice. So, be honest, positive, open and excited and get them involved. If all is going to plan they will be jumping around, excited by the prospect, looking forward to a brother or sister to play with. Being open with the children you already have is essential to getting this right.

FAMILY AND FRIENDS

Not everyone has the great fortune to come from a loving home. It would be impossible to define the 'perfect' family. In fact, I don't believe such a thing exists. Just as we are all different, so are families. They can be good, bad or ugly, generally a mixture of all three. You are bound to get on with some members of your family better than others. You may not be able to choose your kith and kin but you can decide who to become close to, who to trust and confide in. Over the years you will have developed a good feel for how your family functions, its quirks, habits, secrets and interests.

We all turn to those close to us for advice and support, especially about something as personal and emotional as starting a family via the adoption route. Adoption is an emotive topic and it is only natural to seek out those you can use as a sounding board. You will know who to turn to first – when you're ready. Remember that most people have a view on the subject, and it might not be what you expect. It is best to brace yourself for a mixed reaction to the news of your plans.

While you will get an empathically positive reception from professionals, this may not be the case with family and friends. You may be all fired up with 'go get 'em' feelings about this venture while they might have powerfully negative views, or may even try to put you off the idea of adoption. The key is to be able to listen to and respect other family members' views without reacting. You are in control of your reactions but you may have no influence over the views of others. Who knows, you may be pleasantly surprised. Remember, your decision is yours alone to make. While others are fully entitled to their views, so too are you.

It is more likely that family members and close friends will listen, encourage and support you and perhaps share your excitement. You may, however, come across expressions of disbelief, anxiety, shock and even envy. It is best to take a pragmatic view of the feedback you get. See it as a useful survey of those around you. It will be a strong indicator of who you will be able to turn to in the future. Some of your family or friends may, for example, be dead against what you are doing but will come right once you bring your child home. There will be those who are good at supporting you through the paperwork side of adoption as they have practical skills to offer. Others may be indecisive and unhelpful when it comes to the nuts and bolts of the process but very accommodating and dependable emotionally – the people you go to when you just need a big hug or a shoulder to cry on. Both types of support are priceless. It sounds a bit harsh but you are going to need them so it is wise to know who can do what. See those around you as a resource and be conscious of the fact that to get the best out of them you must play to their strengths.

Supportive families will have been with you through the trials and tribulations of your journey towards becoming adoptive parents. For example, they may have accompanied you through years of IVF treatment. They will have witnessed your anguish when it failed time and again. They will have been there when the reality of being childless set in, sharing your natural grief. They will have also been witness to, and possibly part of, your move towards adopting. Perhaps they were a major influence, encouraging you not to give up on a family but to go down this route. They may see it as something incredibly positive, feeding that upbeat energy back to you, making you feel this is something you can do, especially with their love and support. If you have people around you like this then you are blessed indeed, for they will see you through the rough patches ahead and share the joy when things go well. They are your bedrock, and their contribution to this venture will be immeasurable. Count yourself lucky as not everyone has that kind of support from their family. And your adoptive child will benefit enormously by coming into such a solid and loving environment.

Whatever the level of involvement your family has in your decision to adopt, your social worker will want to understand and develop a picture of how you and they interact, and how this will affect any child you adopt. It is not the number of family members available to support you that counts, but the quality of those relationships. In reality, a few good solid relationships are likely to be easier to manage; too many may lead to confusion from too much information.

Sibling relationships

Relationships with siblings are likely to have been affected by your inability to have a child naturally. You may sometimes have felt envious of your brothers and sisters because they have their own children. It is best to acknowledge such feelings, at least to yourself, but it is even better if you can discuss this with your siblings. This may be a tall order given some of the emotions involved. It is important to 'own' the emotions. They are real and they are yours. To cover them up risks them festering in some dark corner of your mind and popping up when you don't want them to, such as when things aren't going as you may wish. The way of dealing with such hidden things is to take them out, look at them, keep the things you want and discard the rest. Secrets can, and do, create all sorts of difficulties, so be as open to yourself and those who care for you as you can. After all, you have taken matters into your own hands and will become a parent yourself so now is a good time to grow out of sibling rivalries. See this as an opportunity to get closer to your siblings – your child's aunties and uncles. They can have a significant role in all your lives. If they already have children they will be able to guide you or give you advice, even if you do have to grit your teeth from time to time. The benefits of pulling siblings into your new world are likely to be many, so weigh this up by looking at the pros and cons of having them on board. If the question of siblings proves to be a problem then talk it through with your social worker.

It is also worth remembering that you and your siblings may not see your collective upbringing in the same way. The result will be a different perspective on what your family represents. It will affect the ties you have. This is something that may reveal itself during the adoption process. Siblings will either be there for you and prove worthy of the trust you have invested in them, or they will fail you at your time of need. If the latter is the case, treat it as an important lesson. There are others you will be able to turn to. You don't have to get on with your brothers and sisters.

Alternatively, if siblings prove their worth, the adoption process may bring you closer together. Going through something so emotional is the time when the quality of relationships is put to the test. As with all things, honesty and openness are the best policy. It is crucial to know the truth on as many levels as possible. You want to be certain that those you rely on are really there for you. Going through the adoption process provides a good opportunity to mend damaged relationships. You can rebuild them with a view to sharing your new future and working together on raising your children. You will all benefit from a more cohesive, wider family unit.

Dealing with difficult family relationships

It could be that you have little or no contact with your family. Perhaps you do not get on with your parents or close relatives. You may be estranged for various reasons. The agency will know about fractured families; after all, that is their field of expertise. You may be anxious about revealing problems within your family. You might feel it reflects badly on your own ability to parent. However, I cannot emphasise too strongly that it is best for you to be frank and honest with your social worker. You will not be judged harshly on the bad behaviour of others. Tell them your story. It will count against you if they discover at a later date that you have covered matters up.

The social worker needs to build a picture from people who have known you for the longest. Invariably, these will be family members. If they are not available for the assessment the agency will want to know why. You could find this period of scrutiny a useful opportunity to deal with long-buried issues. It will be of great benefit for you to lay any mental ghosts to rest. You may even find yourself feeling strong enough to re-engage in lost relationships. It is a shame how a few bitter words can lead to rifts that run for years and years. Involving a social worker and listening to their experienced guidance may give you the courage to readdress this loss, or at least put it behind you.

PERSONALITY TRAITS AND DISORDERS

Children require safety and boundaries. Therefore they need stable emotional environments. Parents who exhibit rapid mood swings and unpredictable behaviours will interfere with the healthy emotional and intellectual development of their child. Agencies look, and seek evidence, for emotionally stable individuals whose worlds are not disproportionately self-centred. They want people who possess a maturity of outlook; those who recognise the realities of the world and its shortcomings and have healthy coping strategies to deal with life's stressful events. We all have our breaking points but robustness of personality is highly desirable, if not essential, in child-rearing. Your drives and motivations reveal information about your personality, experience, beliefs and passions.

Difficult personality characteristics in parents that can interfere with the process of adoption include:

➤ heightened sensitivity to criticism and setbacks
➤ unforgiving nature that bears grudges
➤ resentful and quarrelsome nature
➤ tendency to blame others for things that go wrong
➤ selfishness, excessive self-focus and self-importance
➤ secretiveness and emotional coldness
➤ limited capacity to express emotion towards others
➤ insensitivity and irresponsibility in behaviour
➤ aggression with outbursts of violence or threats of violence towards oneself or others
➤ insecurity and excessive need for reassurance
➤ low tolerance for frustration
➤ excessive impulsivity
➤ a history of unstable and intense relationships
➤ extreme doubt or caution; indecisiveness
➤ rigidity of thought; stubbornness
➤ pronounced perfectionism
➤ pervasive tension or apprehension
➤ tendency to avoid taking responsibility and be unduly compliant to others' wishes

If your negative personality traits outweigh the positive you are unlikely to be able to provide the right emotional environment for an adopted child. If you have been given a diagnosis of a personality disorder, adoption agencies are unlikely to accept you as an adoptive parent. This is because personality disorders cause problems for those who possess them and those with whom they come into contact. Your adoption agency will want to be assured that a child placed with you will be safe.

EMOTIONS AND RELATIONSHIPS

During the assessment you will be looking at your relationships, how events have moulded them and how you manage the positive and negative events that life throws up in the past, present and in your new future family.

Feelings are your unique subjective experience of emotion. Emotions are the agitated condition or state triggered by a life event, for example hearing that a family member or close friend has died or been injured. You will be aware that the impact of this experience for you will differ from hearing about the death or injury of a stranger. Our emotions generally do not interfere with our ability to run our lives for more than short periods of time. The way we react emotionally to stressful life events is influenced by numerous personal and social factors such as our temperament, the support and practical help available to us, as well as how we have managed similar situations in the past.

How we interpret the 'meaning' of an event lies at the root of how we experience it. Our interpretation will be influenced by many factors. These include genetic blessings and curses, our upbringing, education and intelligence as well as the positive and negative outcomes of our life experiences to date. Our mental state at the time we experience events also colours how we perceive them. For example, we are more likely to be negatively affected by things if we are exhausted, or if we are trying to deal with a number of events at the same time, particularly if we feel we don't have much control over what is happening or if we're depressed.

During the course of your journey to becoming an adoptive parent you are likely to feel a wide range of emotions. These may include joy, anger, fear, sadness, surprise, interest, contempt and even disgust. Each emotion will bring with it traces of your past as there seems to be a sort of emotional superhighway which can whisk you back to your childhood, sometimes quite unexpectedly. Your memories, events and emotions can be triggered through experiences in the present, occasionally in a most unexpected and powerful way. Emotions tell us things about ourselves and other people, and children are very sensitive in this regard.

This chapter has raised many issues that you will probably be considering as you think about whether adoption is the right step for you. You should now have a clearer idea of the sort of person adoption agencies are looking for. Give yourself time to reflect on some of the issues raised here, such as your motivations for adopting. Remember that adoption is an irreversible step so you must be absolutely sure that it is the right one for you at the moment. If you are unsure, use the guidelines given in the chapter to find out as much as you can from as many different people and sources as possible. The pathway to adoption can be emotionally challenging, so don't neglect the emotional impact of adoption on yourself and those close to you.

This first step is primarily about scrutinising your thoughts and emotions, making absolutely sure that you want to go ahead with adoption. It is also about gauging the feelings of those around you, as their love and support is essential. Once you are certain that the emotional foundations are sound, you are ready to look more closely at the nitty-gritty of the process.

CHAPTER 2

Adoption Today

What do we mean when we talk about 'family'? It may sound like a simple enough question. Most of us would start with the Adam and Eve scenario; there is a father who is male and a mother, female. They have children. In our society the immediate family group includes grandparents, aunts, uncles, nieces and nephews.

Not that many years ago you would have been pretty much on the mark with that definition. Today, though, our society has changed. Family is no longer that clearly defined group of people. There is nothing 'simple' about the make-up of the contemporary family – quite the contrary. There are numerous reasons for this, such as divorce and remarriage, single parenting and the social and legal acceptance of homosexuality. This has had a knock-on effect when it comes to adoption. Now the emphasis is less on the appearance of the family a child is placed with and more on their expected level of care and competence.

It may sound odd, but adoption isn't what it used to be. This is a good thing: the changes in legislation have meant that adoption is now open to a much wider cross section of the population. There are more routes to adoption than ever before and it is worth considering which one suits you. In this chapter we will look at today's different types of adoptive families, including single-parent families and same-sex couples. We will also examine the various options that exist for adoption, including adopting from abroad. Alternatives to adoption, such as fostering, will also be discussed.

STEP-PARENT ADOPTION

In England and Wales step-parent adoptions make up nearly one in three of all adoptions but most step-parents do not adopt. The most important thing to bear in mind about step-parent adoption is that the courts will view the whole process from the point of view of the child alone. They will need to be convinced that such a move is in the best interests of the child, both now and in the future, as it removes parental responsibility from a biological parent or someone for whom it has been granted through the courts. It also overturns orders such as Contact Orders, Residence Orders and Special Guardianship Orders. For these reasons the courts require local authorities to interview not only your child but also those with parental responsibility, as well as siblings and other important people in your child's life likely to be affected by this adoption, such as grandparents. If you do not have written consent to proceed with your application for adoption from everyone with parental responsibility for your child, you are likely to require legal advice from a solicitor experienced in these matters.

The first thing to do is to speak to your local social services about your intentions. They are likely to encourage you to consider legal options short of adoption that will grant you parental responsibility. These include a Parental Responsibility Order (through the courts) or Agreement (with your partner) and a Residence Order which, when granted, provides parental responsibility to the holder for the lifetime of the order. These orders benefit your child by relieving them of having to agree to a decision that will legally sever them from their other birth family, and does not remove parental responsibility from their other birth parent.

It will be important that the courts know you have discussed the ramifications of adoption with your child. The social worker responsible for providing a report for the courts will need to provide evidence that your child is fully aware (in an age-appropriate way) of the truth about their origins and relationships within the family. Part of the assessment will also explore what steps you will take to ensure your child has a record of their early life in the same way that any other adoption assessment would require.

You are able to apply to the courts to adopt if:

➤ you are aged 21 or over
➤ you are married to, or living in an enduring family relationship with, the birth parent
➤ you reside in the UK or have been habitually resident here for a year
➤ the child is not yet 18
➤ you have informed the local authority in writing of your intention to apply to court for an Adoption Order
➤ you have lived with the child continually for at least six months

After speaking to your local social services you will need to tell your local council that you plan to adopt at least three months before starting the application with the courts. It is worth checking with your local social services how long this may take; it can be as long as a year. In England and Wales you must obtain an application form (858) from your local magistrates' or county court, complete the form in triplicate and return it with the appropriate fee and additional papers as required. The court will then ask your local authority to provide a report by a social worker. Remember, the courts will only grant an Adoption Order if they believe it to be in the best interests over the lifetime of your child.

KINSHIP ADOPTION

Since time immemorial, kinship care has been the main way people care for their relatives' children in time of crisis or need. If a child has to be away from their birth parents, it makes sense that the first option for their care should be within their family circle. Good kinship care can provide stability, continuity and cultural appropriateness. Bad kinship care can, however, continue to provide just more of the same dysfunctional parenting. Kinship care means that parental responsibility remains with the parents unless directed otherwise by a Court. Special Guardianship Orders, while falling short of adoption, can be empowering, and government legislation encourages the extended family to seek such an order if they feel it is in the child's best interest (see page 68).

As with step-parent adoption, your child is likely to have been living with you for a period of time before you think about adoption. Again, as with step-parent adoption, you will need to speak to your local authority to find out the correct procedures and legal requirements, and to inform them of your decision to adopt. It is likely that the child will have to have lived with you for three out of the previous five years, although this need not have been continuous. The courts will want to be assured that adoption with you is in the child's best interests. They will seek information to allow them to decide in your favour. This will be based on a full assessment carried out by a social worker, for which you may have to pay. Just as with any other adoption situation, ongoing support is important to ensure the success of kinship adoption.

SINGLE-PARENT ADOPTION

Single parents are able to adopt children and can make excellent parents. Indeed, single parents may be particularly beneficial to some children who have difficulties relating to more than one person at any one time and may have been traumatised in the past. Just like every other adoptive parent you will be thoroughly assessed. Particular attention will be paid to your competences, resilience and the social networks and support that will be available for you and your child during placement and beyond. Being a parent is a tough job; being a single parent is no less a challenge.

LESBIAN AND GAY ADOPTION

The desire to parent is universal and independent of sexual orientation and gender. In the past, homosexual individuals and couples were prevented from being considered as adoptive parents for numerous reasons. In some cases this related to firmly held religious beliefs, but in others it was the product of ignorance and bigotry. There was a feeling that gay men and lesbians somehow corrupt their children; that they are paedophiles preying on vulnerable children, and therefore incapable of being good parents. Paedophilia has nothing to do with sexual orientation. For example, in a 1994 study[5] of 269 individuals who were sexually abused as children, 267 of the abusers were heterosexual; only two were identified as homosexual. Children are much more likely to be abused by heterosexual partners or relatives than individuals identified as homosexual.

Lesbian and gay applicants are likely to have overcome discrimination in many forms. This may place them in an excellent position to understand children who have experienced unfairness and intolerance. The qualities and abilities to be a good parent are not related to sexual orientation or gender. Studies into lesbian or gay parenting have yet to identify harmful effects on children placed with these individuals or couples. Research shows 'no differences in any measures between heterosexual and homosexual parents regarding parenting styles, emotional adjustment and sexual orientation of the children'.[6]

Lesbians or lesbian couples have the possibility of creating their own child or adopting. Gay men can, of course, sire children by donating sperm, and some lesbian and gay couples have come to some such arrangements. Nevertheless, adoption is a common first choice for lesbians, and is perhaps the only choice for male couples and single gay men. Homosexual individuals who apply to become adoptive parents on their own are more likely to have difficulties related to being a single parent than regarding their sexual orientation.

You may find it difficult to be honest about your sexual orientation when contemplating applying to become an adoptive parent because you are anxious about jeopardising your chances of being accepted. Before you apply, it is therefore essential to ask your local adoption agency or voluntary agency about their policy regarding gay and lesbian adopters. Most will be happy to provide you with this information and you should not be put off applying. Some local authorities may not advertise or promote their services to lesbian and gay individuals or couples in order to prevent criticism and perhaps to maintain funding, or may have come under direct political pressure. While overt or more subtle discrimination may remain in some quarters, remember, it is not legal.

You will obviously want to be honest with your child about your situation, discussing it with them at a level appropriate for their age. This will be important, particularly in relation to how they describe their family when they are at school. Talking about your family and sharing details of its structure with other children is part of the educational process, and so it will be with your child. Obviously, you will be involved in choosing your child's school and will want to be involved in all aspects of their educational development. Part of your parental role will be to speak with your child's teacher, perhaps even the headteacher, to get a feel for how their school approaches issues of sexuality and what, in negotiation with you, is the best way to manage this issue for your child. The educational establishment in the UK seems to have moved forwards positively in understanding and managing children from a wide variety of unique and ever-changing backgrounds. You will be right to expect a sympathetic and supportive ear as both you and your child's teachers will want the best for your child.

Honesty is generally the best policy. Truthfulness and sincerity must form the bedrock of your relationship with your child, and will influence their future stability, happiness and emotional and intellectual development. It will be difficult to build a relationship with your child without this integrity and openness. You have nothing to be ashamed of and you can make good parents. Your rights to do this are now enshrined in the law.

If your sexual orientation has distanced you from various members of your close or extended family, your decision to adopt may act to heal rifts. Becoming a parent may lead you to a greater understanding of your relationship with your parents; it may even bring you closer together. You might, for example, be providing them with one of their most cherished wishes – a grandchild.

During the assessment process your family and friends will be involved. The adoption agency will seek information about your character and personal habits from people who have known you for the longest time. Clearly, your family will fall into this category but you may be anxious if your network of friends is overwhelmingly lesbian or gay. Although such anxiety is only natural, remember that your abilities to be a good parent are nothing to do with your sexuality whatsoever. Adoption agencies are interested in finding out about you and how you are likely to parent a child, about your strengths, your motivations and your determination to care for your child, and they will need to get this information, just as for any heterosexual couple or single parent, from people who have known you over time. Your network of friends is important for your emotional wellbeing and therefore, directly and/or indirectly, for the emotional wellbeing of your child. Remember too: you have the law on your side.

The assessment will require information about how you relate to children and the child-rearing experiences you may have had, such as with any nieces and nephews. It is useful to talk to other lesbian or gay couples who have been down this route about their experiences in and understanding of child-rearing. You will also find it helpful to talk to others who have nieces and nephews and pick their brains. As with all sources of information, some will prove more important and beneficial to you than others.

Whoever you are and whatever your orientation, you are entitled to the same courtesy, information and support as any other applicant considering becoming an adoptive parent. You will want to go through the same assessment procedure as everyone else as it will be important for you to know that you are being judged by the same standards of potential parenting skills. When you finish, you will therefore be confident that you have been judged to be potentially good-enough parents. You will surmount an equal number of hurdles, if not more. Determination and tenacity are important and you will require a good support network, just like anyone else.

You can expect your social worker to have moved beyond any stereotypes they may hold. They should seek evidence of, and examine dispassionately, your competences, strengths and limitations, as they are legally required to do for all applicants. As with heterosexual applicants, the focus will be on your relationships in the past and present. Your upbringing will be explored, together with evidence of how you have coped with adversity in the past. It may be difficult for your social worker and you if you are in any way unsure of your own situation – for example, if you're not fully 'out'. As with most things in adoption, if you are unsure it is best to seek advice. Ask your adoption agency or contact organisations such as Stonewall, Adoption UK or the Post-adoption Centre (see Resources, page 248).

INTERCOUNTRY ADOPTION

There are many reasons why individuals contemplate adopting from abroad. As there are few babies needing adoption in the UK, possibly the most important reason for choosing to adopt from abroad is the desire to adopt a baby or infant. Alternatively, there may be cultural or family connections to a particular country. Other reasons include altruism. Few cannot be touched by the plight of children in disaster-torn or famine-ravished countries and want to reach out to offer orphaned children a better start in life.

In 2007, the number of intercountry adoption cases dealt

with by the Intercountry Adoption Casework Team at the Department for Children, Schools and Families (DCSF) was 356. Over the past six years the average number has been about 330. Intercountry adoption is expensive and complicated. It is best to get advice from agencies, either voluntary or local authority, that specialise or have expertise in overseas adoption. It is essential that you work with bona fide, established, professional organisations and do not try to cut corners. If all of the legal and bureaucratic hurdles have not been properly negotiated, you can end up paying more and delaying the whole process. It is important to have a written breakdown of costs and to be able to develop trust with your agency, lawyers and others involved. You can find out about the legal requirements and procedures for most countries from the DCSF (www.dcsf.gov.uk).

You will have to pay for your assessment. This is unlikely to be less than £5,000. Other costs include return travel to your child's country; hotel and food expenses; fees to your adoption agency; your lawyer's fees; fees to notarise numerous documents as well as the costs of the documents themselves, such as court fees and fees for nationality. Certain countries may have their own particular costs which you will need to ascertain from the local adoption agency or possibly the embassy of the country from which you wish to adopt. Make sure you are aware of roughly how much you may have to pay before you commit to this course of action.

The bureaucracy you have to go through is extensive and time-consuming. The whole process can take two to three years or more. It is also worth remembering that children from other countries face the same disadvantages that children for adoption in the UK have experienced in terms of psychological and emotional upheaval, neglect, abuse and trauma. Children from abroad may also have spent more time in orphanages and be institutionalised. There may be physical handicaps and you may be less likely to know if there are any developmental or psychological handicaps. In essence, the challenges are the same as adopting children in the UK but complicated by culture, language and unavailable or unreliable knowledge about your child's previous life.

You will have to go through the same adoption assessment as in the UK with added attention paid to:

➤ how you will help your child adjust to a new language and culture
➤ what provision you will make to ensure your child is made aware of their cultural heritage
➤ why you have chosen to adopt from this particular country

You will have to satisfy not only those who are assessing you in the UK but also those involved in the process from your child's country. Only those local authorities or voluntary adoption agencies registered to work on intercountry adoptions can undertake your assessment.

Once you have been approved by an adoption panel, the information is passed to the DCSF and the Intercountry Adoption Casework Team. They will need to satisfy themselves that all of the documentation has been appropriately completed and satisfies UK legislation. Once they are content that the application is legal and complete, they will issue a Certificate of Eligibility and Suitability to Adopt. You must have this certificate before you are able to bring a child into the UK for adoption.

Your papers will then have to meet the legal and procedural requirements of the country you are adopting from, and this is likely to require further administrative and bureaucratic formalities. When all of this is completed the Intercountry Adoption Casework Team will send your papers to the appropriate authority in your child's country. It is considered unwise to look for a child in your chosen country before you get the 'all clear'. This is to avoid the dreadful situation of having to return to the UK without the child for a number of months while assessment is carried out and your application is processed, and without the certainty that you will be approved. Some countries forbid anyone to identify a child without having been assessed and approved in the UK first.

Once your chosen country has received the paperwork from the DCSF they will start to look for a match for you. This can take anything up to two years, depending on the country you are adopting from. The DCSF, your lawyer or adoption agency should be able to advise you in more detail of the procedures that will be required once a match has been made. You will need to travel to meet your child before things can progress. Procedures vary in different countries but there will usually be an adoption hearing at a court in your child's country. If all goes well you then have to negotiate bringing your child back to the UK.

Once you have adopted your child you may need to make what is known as an Entry Clearance Application at the embassy, consulate or high commission nearest to where your child is living. This is dealt with by the Entry Clearance Officer who will check all the paperwork relating to your child and how they became available for adoption as well as all your paperwork (again). Any inconsistencies or concerns will be investigated. The information you require includes:

➤ the child's original and new birth certificates
➤ parental consent (or a certificate of abandonment from the relevant authorities)
➤ an Adoption/Guardianship Order (or if there is no such order, written permission from the relevant authorities of the country concerned that they are content for the child to leave the country and travel to the UK to be adopted)
➤ a recent medical report on the child
➤ if the child is seven or over, a report of the interview with the child in which their view and understanding of the proposed adoption is clearly recorded

All of these documents must be translated into English if necessary. They must also be notarised, which means the documents and signatures have to be authenticated by a legally authorised Notary (Public) whose fees you will have to pay.

In 1993, the Hague Convention on the Protection of Children and co-operation in respect of intercountry adoption set out to prevent the abduction of, the sale of and illegal trafficking in children. The Convention requires that intercountry adoption happens only when it is in the child's best interests; that all adopters are properly assessed and approved as suitable to adopt and no profit is made from the process. Adoption from a country that has implemented the Hague Convention means that a child will automatically receive British citizenship (if you or your partner are a British citizen and both of you are habitually resident in the UK). The adoption is automatically recognised not only in the UK but also in other countries that are signatories to the Hague Convention. Your adoption agency should be able to tell you whether the country from which you wish to adopt a child is a Hague Convention country or not, and if it is on the Designated List (the list of countries that are named on the Adoption [Designation of Overseas Adoptions] Order 1973). The UK automatically recognises an adoption made in any of the countries named on the Designated List. An up-to-date list of these countries can be found on the website of the Department for Children, Schools and Families: www.dcsf.gov.uk

---

Hague Convention signatories include: Albania, Australia, Austria, Belarus, Bolivia, Brazil, Bulgaria, Burkina Faso, Burundi, Canada, Chile, Colombia, Costa Rica, Cyprus, Czech Republic, Denmark, Ecuador, El Salvador, Estonia, Finland, Georgia, Germany, Iceland, India, Israel, Italy, Latvia, Lithuania, Luxembourg, Mauritius, Mexico, Moldova, Monaco, Mongolia, Netherlands, New Zealand, Norway, Panama, Paraguay, Peru, Philippines, Poland, Romania, Slovakia, Slovenia, South Africa, Spain, Sri Lanka, Sweden, Switzerland, United Kingdom, Uruguay and Venezuela.

The Designated List includes the Commonwealth countries of: Anguilla, Australia, Bahamas, Barbados, Belize, Bermuda, Botswana, British Virgin Islands, Canada, Cayman Islands, Cyprus, Dominica, Fiji, Ghana, Gibraltar, Guyana, Hong Kong, Jamaica, Kenya, Lesotho, Malawi, Malaysia, Malta, Mauritius, Montserrat, Namibia, New Zealand, Nigeria, Pitcairn Island, St Christopher and Nevis, St Vincent, Seychelles, Singapore, South Africa, Sri Lanka, Swaziland, Tanzania, Tonga, Trinidad and Tobago, Uganda, Zambia, Zimbabwe, and foreign countries: Austria, Belgium, China, Denmark (including Greenland and the Faroes), Finland, France (including Reunion, Martinique, Guadeloupe and French Guyana), Germany, Greece, Iceland, the Republic of Ireland, Israel, Italy, Luxembourg, The Netherlands (including the Antilles), Norway, Portugal (including the Azores and Madeira), Spain (including the Balearics and Canary Islands), Surinam, Sweden, Switzerland, Turkey and the United States of America.

You can adopt from a country that is not a Hague Convention country, but the Adoption Order from that country is not recognised in the UK and you will need to adopt your child in a UK court for the adoptive relationship to be legally recognised. You must notify your local authority within 14 days of bringing your child into the UK and inform them whether or not you intend to adopt the child and provide them with a home. The child will have to live with you in the UK for at least six months before you are able to apply to adopt your child. (You do not have to notify your local authority if you have adopted from a country on the Designated List, but you are advised to do so as you and your child are entitled to post-adoption support.) After you have adopted your child, most countries require a progress report to be sent to them at regular intervals. These will be completed by your local authority or voluntary adoption agency registered to work with intercountry adoptions. The frequency of these reports will be dictated by the country from which you have adopted your child.

It all sounds rather confusing, and you will need professional help and advice as well as advice from others who have gone through this procedure. The law relating to intercountry adoption is The Adoption (Bringing Children into the United Kingdom) Regulations Statutory Instrument 2003 No. 1173 and is available online or in published form.[7]

PARENTING OTHER THAN ADOPTING

FOSTERING

Foster parenting is shared care between you, the local authority and the biological parent(s). It is exceptionally worthwhile and generally short term, with nearly three-quarters of children returning to their biological families within a year. Although you do not have parental responsibility you have a vital role in helping children through crises, and the relationship that develops between you can be extremely important to your child. You will have to go through an assessment process similar to adoption and be recommended by a fostering panel before a child is placed with you. You will be paid an allowance to cover day-to-day essentials and for looking after your child. Support will be provided by local authority social workers, including regular training and meetings with other foster carers locally.

A few children need long-term fostering. Sometimes it becomes apparent with the passage of time that a child would benefit from being adopted. You may consider applying to adopt your child, and should discuss this with your social worker. If the child is going to be adopted by someone else, your role is vital in ensuring as smooth a transition as possible. The information you will be able to provide, for both your child and the adoptive parents, will be invaluable.

RESIDENCE AND SPECIAL GUARDIANSHIP ORDERS

A Residence Order gives shared responsibility for the care of a child, often in cases involving relatives or foster carers. It can also clarify where a child will live if parents are separating and there is some disagreement. (See also Kinship Adoption, page 54.)

The Special Guardianship Order came into being under the Adoption and Children Act 2002. A halfway house between a Residence Order and an Adoption Order, it provides another legal option for children who cannot grow up with their birth families. The special guardian is given parental responsibility for the child until they are 18. While it does not remove all responsibility from the birth parents, it does limit their ability to exercise control over the child. The special guardian has to consult with them about decisions only in exceptional circumstances.

In some ways a Special Guardianship Order is more akin to adoption than other types of order as it is difficult to end or discharge. The matter would have to be put before the courts and would be agreed only if there were dramatic changes in the situation that would affect the welfare of the child. Special guardianship is a serious commitment. Like adoption, it aims to protect children and provide them with security, and gives parents the necessary autonomy to promote good parenting. The special guardian has responsibility for the day-to-day care of the child or young person. They will make all the key decisions on issues such as schooling.

The order makes the care arrangements more legally secure than a Residence Order. It enables the child to maintain stronger links with their birth family than if they were adopted. Their legal identity does not change and they are still known by the name of their birth family. They cannot be made to change their surname or taken out of the country for more than three months at a time without permission from the courts and the biological parent/s.[8]

This chapter has outlined not only the various types of adoption available, but also parenting options short of adoption. Knowing what choice is available is crucial in weighing up what to do next. The next step is the big one: applying to be considered as an adoptive parent and all that follows from that decision.

PART TWO:
APPLICATION, ASSESSMENT
AND ACCEPTANCE

CHAPTER 3

The Adoption Process

Let's get started. This chapter will introduce you to the information adoption agencies are required to obtain, the professionals who will work with you in your endeavour, and what part they play in organising your passage towards acceptance as an adoptive parent.

From the moment you apply to be considered as an adoptive parent you set in motion a clearly defined and well-documented sequence of events. This procedure has evolved over the years and aims to make the tricky business of matching a child with a family as successful as possible for all parties concerned. You must always bear in mind that the child comes first in this process – decisions are made for the benefit of the child ahead of everyone else. The people who assess you need to collect as much information as they can about you. At times the questions asked will feel unnecessarily intrusive, possibly irrelevant or even stupid. However, there is method in what may seem like a touch of madness.

It is essential for you to have a clear grasp of how the adoption process works and what to expect. In this chapter, for the sake of clarity, I will break it down into its component parts. I will explain in more detail who can adopt and the key individuals you will be dealing with, and provide a guide to the procedures you will encounter.

THE FIRST STEPS

Once you have taken that first scary step, usually by picking up the phone and calling a local authority or agency, the system is designed to give you the maximum support available. You should receive written information in the post, and will be invited to go to a meeting or be offered the chance for a social worker to visit your home to talk through adoption with you. These first tentative meetings are crucial as it is now that you will have the opportunity to test yourself to see if you really are serious about adopting.

Generally, the next stage is for you to be asked to attend a series of sessions that prepare you for the process. You will meet people who have successfully adopted and have the chance to learn from their experiences. You will also come face to face with other people like yourself. These encounters should help make you feel that you are not alone. Although you might be a little shy at first, these adoption preparation groups are a valuable source of support and strength. Most people come away from them feeling empowered and ready for the fray. (See 'Study Groups', Chapter 1, pages 33–37.)

Once you have made a formal application, a case record will be opened for you called the Prospective Adopters' Report. In the fullness of time this will include:

➤ your application
➤ information and reports obtained by the agency
➤ your Home Study
➤ your observations on the Home Study

➤ historical record of the agency's decisions
➤ a record of the adoption panel's proceedings
➤ recommendations and any advice given to the agency

If the prospective adopter has previously applied to the Secretary of State for a review by an Independent Review Panel, their recommendations will be in this report, as will your observations on the recommendations. The Prospective Adopters' Report will also contain any other documents or information obtained by the agency that it considers relevant.

Right at the very beginning of the process, after or even just before you fill in your formal application, you are likely to be asked to give consent for the agency to carry out police CRB (Criminal Records Bureau) checks. Your adoption agency is required by law to do this. These are called enhanced criminal record certificates and apply to you and any other member in the household aged 18 years or over. (For more information, see 'The Legal Profession', page 90.)

Your health is an important factor so the agency will obtain a written report from your doctor. This should include:

➤ your age, sex, weight and height
➤ your health history, including details of any serious physical or mental illness, disability, accident, hospital admission or attendance at an outpatient department, and in each case any treatment given
➤ details of any present illness, including treatment and prognosis

➤ information on infertility or reasons for deciding not to have children
➤ your obstetric history
➤ details of any consumption of alcohol, cigarettes and habit-forming drugs
➤ your family's health history, including details of any serious physical or mental illness or hereditary disease or disorder among your brothers and sisters and children
➤ any other relevant information that may assist the panel and agency in their deliberations

(For more information on the health assessment, see Chapter 4, page 97.)

The adoption process may run into problems early on. Some problems may be rectifiable. For example, you may have to move because of a change in your family circumstances, or you may be having second thoughts. In these situations you will be able to reapply to be considered at a later date. Some problems, however, may be inflexible. For instance, you may develop a terminal medical condition or your CRB check may throw up something untoward. If you encounter any such problems or pitfalls during the process, your social worker will be able to advise you and give you all the information you need.

WHO'S WHO IN YOUR ASSESSMENT

ADOPTION AGENCIES

Adoption agencies need to be able to entrust a child with you for the rest of that child's life. They will therefore expect you to be honest with them from the outset. You can expect the same from them. Adoption and fostering services are required to conform to minimum standards. Agencies are inspected at regular intervals to ensure standards are upheld.

Agencies' responsibilities include trying to determine a child's birth parents' desires and feelings about their child's adoption. They then try their best to place a child taking into account these wishes, as well as issues relating to a child's religion, racial origin and language. Adoption agencies are required to prepare an adoption placement report and agree this with you before matching you with a child. They have to visit you at statutory intervals following the placement of your child and they must provide the necessary reports for court. At all times they must be able to explain why they believe their decisions are in the best interests of the child.

Adoptive parents do have a choice as to where to 'take their business'. While it is the statutory responsibility of local authorities to take children into care and seek adoption where necessary, you don't have to apply to them. You can opt for a voluntary agency as you may feel you will get a more personal, tailored service. Such agencies are often in an excellent position to provide post-placement support for you. The drawback is that this might limit your choice. In the race to adopt, local authorities who select or approve their own applicants are likely to give them 'first choice' of children in their care before offering a child to a voluntary agency for placement. This is more likely to occur if the authority is having difficulties placing a particular child or children. Agencies can differ greatly and it is worth shopping around to see what is available in your locality. You can find details of agencies through the British Association for Adoption and Fostering (BAAF). Try its helpful website (see Resources, page 248).

Not all agencies accept every application. Some are small and specialise in particular areas. You can turn this to your advantage, though, by seeking an agency that matches your sexual, cultural, ethnic or spiritual values and background. It may be that a voluntary agency will allow you more flexibility and choice, particularly if you have something specific to offer such as a religion or language, or you might be able to care for a child with special needs.

It's usually best to go with the option that will make the process easiest for you. Your choice of agency may be limited by a number of factors. One of these is geography. Some agencies have a limit on the distances they will travel so will only accept applicants within a certain radius. This is likely to be for purely practical reasons, relating to the problems of organising home assessments. As you will be attending educational events, the question of distance is one that you too should take into account. It may also alter the amount of post-adoption support available. Local authorities have the benefit of being just that – local. This means they will provide post-adoption services for you and your child or children as near your own doorstep as possible. By choosing a local agency, distances involved in visits and contact are greatly simplified, and much cheaper. If you go the local authority route and they decide to accept you as an adoptive parent, their preference will be to match you with a child nearby.

It's also important to get a feel for the likely timescale to expect from particular agencies. These and other issues will inform your choice of agency. You are at the beginning of a long journey, one that will have a permanent impact on the lives of all those involved. Getting the right agency is of the utmost importance as you will not be allowed to run two assessments concurrently.

You may find that your initial approaches to an agency are unsuccessful. This could be for a number of reasons. An agency may not be taking new cases at the time of your application because of the high number of approved adopters on their books already. The type of children available for adoption at an agency might not match what you feel able to manage, or there may be difficulties with the numbers of trained staff available to undertake assessments. The message is clear: shop around and contact a number of agencies before settling on one.

The professionals involved should make you feel welcome and comfortable. You should feel that you are being taken seriously and listened to, and this should be obvious from the first contact you have with an agency. It is a good idea to speak to adoptive parents who have been through the process with your chosen agency and are willing to share their experiences. The testament of adoptive parents ought to be a very powerful and encouraging endorsement of an agency.

From the outset the adoption agency should be able to allay your fears or anxieties and gently dispel any fantasies you may have about choosing to adopt. The assessment process should be the beginning of sharing your thoughts and experiences with others seeking to embark on this journey and those who have already started the process. In an ideal scenario, this process can be one of the most empowering and useful experiences, setting the scene for adoption in a most positive way. It should reassure you that you're doing the right thing and, although the child's needs are paramount throughout, without you they may not get a future family.

Remember, adoption is an intricate endeavour involving lots of people. It is not like a simple problem-solving task. No matter how much you will want to roll up your sleeves and 'get on with it', you will need patience. The initial, and future, contact with adoption agencies is all about giving and receiving information. Everyone is trying to ensure a child placed with you will be safe, and that you are provided with enough information and support to make a success of the match. Assessment is not personal; it's legal. Most adopting parents hang on to this thought when, or if, the going gets tough.

YOUR SOCIAL WORKER

Your main contact with the agency of your choice will be the social worker assigned to your case. They will be experienced in adoption and have had special training in this area. Their role in your adoption process is crucial; they are the eyes and ears of the agency. You need to realise that this will be someone you will get to know very well. They will be spending time in your home, interviewing you and your partner. They will want to know about, and possibly meet, your family and friends. The ideal scenario is for you to develop a good relationship with your social worker, not simply to smooth the path of your application but so that you can benefit from their skills and experience before and after placement.

Social work is a tough job. Placing a child for the rest of their lives with your family is a huge responsibility and an exceedingly delicate and complex undertaking. In adoption, emotions run high as there is so much to gain and potentially so much to lose if things go awry. Few social workers work in this area without an abiding passion to help disadvantaged children. They come under pressure from the legal system, politicians, biological parents, children and those foster carers and adoptive parents for whom they have responsibility. Theirs is not a job for the fainthearted. Social workers will do the best they can to ensure the safety and longevity of the placement of your child. They are, however, only human and cannot achieve miracles; a bit of give and take will be essential on both sides.

Although this process will all be new to you, bear in mind that your social worker will have been through it many times with many people. They should see the potholes long before you fall into them. The social workers I have spoken to tell me that they want adoptive parents to draw on their experience and join with them to ensure the best for their children. If all goes to plan you should feel that you are well informed and being listened to and valued.

Your social worker will prepare the primary report on you, known as the 'Home Study' or 'assessment', which forms the basis of the information that goes before an adoption panel. How long this takes varies between agencies. The legal guidance is that it should take eight months to get from your application to the study being presented to an adoption panel. The social worker will record details about you in the Prospective Adopters' Report, also known as 'Form F'. Of all the bits of paper that will pass under your nose, this one is the most important. Form F pulls together all the information that the powers that be use to decide whether you are right for adoption or not. (A more in-depth look into the way the report is compiled and what the agency is looking for is available online from BAAF, see Resources, page 248.)

In all this your social worker is a key figure as they will be your assessor and, hopefully, your advocate. The better you get on with them the easier this period of scrutiny will be. You might find it difficult to be completely frank and honest with a stranger but if you can nurture this relationship you will get much more out of it. If, on the other hand, you find yourself having problems with the social worker it is important to deal with this early on. Talk it through with them and, if that doesn't help, have a chat with another team member from the agency. If all else fails you can ask to be allocated a different social worker. Remember, though, that your ability to get through relationship difficulties could be viewed as an indicator as to how you might cope when you have the inevitable, and completely normal, run-ins with your adopted child.

ADOPTION PANEL

The Home Study put together by your social worker goes before an adoption panel. This group, set up by the agency or the local authority, holds your fate in its hands. The documentation submitted to them includes the Prospective Adopters' Report, on which they will primarily base their decision. Just to be clear: while the adoption panel is required by law to consider and weigh the evidence, it is the adoption agency's responsibility to make the final determination in your case. In coming to this conclusion, the agency's decision-maker is legally bound to take into account the panel's findings.

You will be invited to meet the panel so it is helpful to understand who you will be dealing with. The panel consists of a maximum of 10 people.

➤ The chair, a person with experience in this field.
➤ Two social workers, each with at least three years' relevant experience after qualifying.
➤ An individual who is involved in management of an adoption agency or a member of the local authority.
➤ A medical adviser.
➤ At least three other people, known as 'independent members', two of whom should have personal experience of adoption.

Members are allowed to sit on the panel for up to three years. The panel requires a quorum of five to six members and keeps a written record of its proceedings. It will take into account all of the information and reports about you. Additionally, it may ask an adoption agency to obtain other relevant information it considers necessary, and may obtain legal advice if it thinks it is needed in a particular case.

The idea of appearing in front of this group may be daunting but the important thing to remember is the very fact you have got this far means the odds are in your favour. If you were really unsuitable to adopt then the social worker would have spotted this much earlier in the process and should have already let you know that there was a problem. By the time you find yourself sitting before the panel all the hard work has been done; they will have all the information they need in the reports set before them. So relax as best you can and hold on to the thought that the panel are not there to give you a grilling. They will be as keen as you are to find a good, loving and stable home for the children who desperately need one.

The panel will be considering a number of key issues. They will want to get a feel for your motivation and emotional wellbeing. They will consider why you want to adopt and how you have dealt with the strong emotions that have preceded this application, such as years of trying for a baby of your own and failed attempts at IVF. Do you have what it takes to get to grips with the emotional needs of the child you will be adopting? How have you dealt with upheavals in previous relationships? Do you have a good support structure around you: family and friends who will be there to lend a hand, both physically and meta-phorically? If you already have children, how will that affect the new addition? There is evidence, for instance, that a placement will be problematic if there is too small an age difference between children already in the family; the panel will therefore look for a gap of at least two years. Like so many factors involved, nothing is cast in stone, and each case is assessed on its merits.

Age is another consideration. Although there is no upper age limit for adoption, the panel will want to be as sure as they can that you will be fit and healthy enough to continue to care for the child they place with you well into their late teens and beyond. Illness and advanced years may therefore work against you here. Conversely, people who have already brought up a family are older but wiser, and that will count in their favour. Once again, each application is different and will be treated on a case-by-case basis.

If all goes well the panel will make a recommendation of acceptance to the adoption agency. They might include more specific details such as their view on the number of children you might be suitable to adopt, their age range, sex, likely needs and background. This information is then passed back to the adoption agency which has the ultimate say in the process.

You will be notified of the result by post. If you are not accepted you have to be given the reasons in writing. The agency has to tell you if its decision is different from the panel's recommendations. You have 40 working days in England, and 28 days in Wales and Scotland, to ask for a review. In England you can appeal to the agency or apply to the Independent Review Mechanism (IRM), a government-funded body run by the BAAF. This is an 'either/or' choice; you cannot do both. In Wales this is known as the Independent Review of Determination and is run by the Welsh Assembly. Similar review is available in Scotland where a number of agencies run a 'reconsideration procedure'. The IRM will ensure that you can put your case before an independent panel. Once again, you will be invited to attend. The IRM will make its own recommendation to your agency, which still makes the final decision, and this time it will be binding. Remember: act within the time period allowed for an appeal or the agency's recommendations will automatically come into force.

Complaints and Appeals

Independent Review Mechanism (IRM)

The IRM is run in England by BAAF under contract to the Department of Children, Schools and Families. If things have not gone your way and your adoption agency has declined to approve you as an adoptive parent, you are entitled to an explanation. This decision by an adoption agency is known as a 'qualifying determination' and is available to both prospective adopters who wish to adopt a child from the UK as well as those adopting from abroad. A qualifying determination may be made during the assessment process or after a full assessment of your suitability to adopt. It can also be made if an adoption agency proposes to withdraw an earlier approval. If not satisfied with this outcome you may use the Independent Review Mechanism. This provides you with the option to have your case reviewed by a totally independent panel; the Independent Review Panel (IRP).

Common reasons for not recommending prospective adopters as suitable include:

➤ medical concerns
➤ withholding important information from the agency
➤ the ability of prospective adopters to work with the agency
➤ information supplied by referees
➤ the psychological capacity to parent or understand the needs of a looked-after child or a child from a different ethnic, religious or cultural background

If information comes to light during the assessment process that raises concerns as to your suitability, the agency should advise you about this. If you then decide not to withdraw your application, the agency will prepare a Brief Prospective Adopters' Report and send it to the adoption panel. They will make a recommendation to the adoption agency's decision-maker who will inform you of their decision.

You must make your application within 40 days (20 working days in Wales) of the date the adoption agency informed you of the qualifying determination. This should give you enough time to reflect and consider what course of action is right for you. For example, you will have to choose whether you will make representations to your adoption agency or apply for a review through the IRM. The Independent Review Panel is not a higher appeals authority and it cannot overturn your adoption agency's final decision. Its role is to make fresh recommendations which your agency's decision-maker has to consider.

If, after taking in the review panel's comments, your agency declines to accept you as an adoptive parent, you have no right of appeal against this decision. You can, however, seek legal advice from a solicitor or Citizens Advice Bureau. In the year 2006/7, adoption agencies' decision-makers agreed with IRP recommendations in over 70 per cent of reviews. In England, IRPs reviewed 25 cases – 18 domestic adoptions and 7 adoptions from abroad. Sixteen applications were from married couples, seven from single people and two from unmarried couples (opposite and same-sex). Of the 25 cases reviewed, 40 per cent were not considered suitable to become adoptive parents; 30 per cent were considered suitable; and in the other 30 per cent it was recommended that the assessment should continue and the Prospective Adopters' Report be completed. It is thus worth seeking a review of your case. Don't give up.

The Independent Review Panel (IRP)
The cost of taking your case to an Independent Review Panel will be met by your adoption agency. The IRP will endeavour to complete your case within four months. The panel will include two social workers, a medical practitioner and up to six other members. All panel members will have some professional or personal experience of adoption; some may be adopters or adopted adults. Each panel will have a written legal report on your case. A professional adviser will be present to provide panel members with advice on legislation, guidance and research in order to

ensure that all relevant issues are considered and correct procedures are followed. The IRP can seek further information from you or your adoption agency as well as legal advice if it thinks it necessary. You can expect to be asked to attend a hearing of up to two hours.

The panel will consider your suitability to adopt in general. It will not, and cannot, make a recommendation in connection with a specific child or deal with complaints against the adoption agency. The function of the panel is to consider the case anew and to make a fresh recommendation to the agency. The agency's decision-maker will then consider both the original panel's recommendation and the review panel's recommendation before coming to a decision. The panels can be held in Manchester, Leeds, Bristol, Birmingham, Cambridge and London. Inter-country adoption cases are held in either London or Manchester. You and your adoption agency will receive a copy of the review panel's recommendation within two weeks of your hearing. Your adoption agency will subsequently write to you to inform you of its final decision. You may seek access to the review panel's minutes in accordance with the Data Protection Act 1998. You are likely to receive an extract from the minutes so that only personal data as defined under the Act is included. (See Resources, page 248, for further information and contact details.)

There is a chance, albeit rare, that the adoption will be contested by the biological parents. This is something that is likely to be apparent from very early on. It should have been anticipated by the powers that be who will have a good knowledge of the family in question. If this does happen you may need to seek legal advice. The whole process may be complicated and more expensive, and will certainly be a much more fraught experience for everyone involved. It will be just as worthwhile; just more of a slog. What you will have on your side, though, is the weight of the authorities and the adoption agency. With their support, both in terms of access to legal advice and emotional propping up, you have a strong team on board to fight for your child. (For further information on contested adoptions, see Chapter 6.)

THE LEGAL PROFESSION

Although you are essentially undergoing a legal process when you adopt, the only time you are likely to come under scrutiny by the law as such is when you are screened to see if you have a criminal record. Becoming an adoptive parent will require what is known as an enhanced CRB check.

The aim is to enhance the safety of children by seeking information on any convictions, cautions, reprimands and warnings in England and Wales, and most of the relevant convictions in Scotland and Northern Ireland. In order to do this, the following sources may be accessed: the Police National Computer, the government's Protection of Children Act and Vulnerable Adults List and, where appropriate, information held under Section 142 of the Education Act 2002 by the Department for Children, Schools and Families. In addition, appropriate information held by local police forces and other agencies relating to relevant non-conviction information may also be sought.

It is important to be honest with your agency about any past criminal convictions. If you have any anxieties about this, you can call the confidential helpline of the National Association for the Care and Resettlement of Offenders (NACRO) for advice. NACRO is a crime-reduction charity that works with ex-offenders (see Resources, page 248).

HEALTH PROFESSIONALS

It is necessary to check that you have no medical or psychiatric conditions that will compromise your child's health, development and wellbeing. The results of your medical examination will go to the agency's medical officer. If you have any worries about your health, it is worth speaking to this person early on. Your social worker will be able to put you in contact.

TEACHERS

You will become involved in your child's schooling and develop a relationship with their teachers. You may or may not meet your child's teacher during the matching and placement process, depending on the age of your child. It will be essential for you to be made fully aware of any educational problems your child might have as early as possible. You will need to be able to talk them through with experts, particularly if your child has recognised special educational needs. A child's learning difficulties sometimes become noticeable later on, but the earlier you can spot them the better. You may have to lobby hard for your child, depending on where you live and what services are available locally.

ORGANISING TIME OFF WORK

In law, just like any biological parent, you are entitled to time off work in order to be with your new child. This is called Statutory Adoption Leave and is equivalent to Maternity Leave. Statutory Paternity Leave is also available (see page 94) and, if you are adopting as a couple, you will need to decide which of you takes what entitlement.

Adoption leave is there to provide you with protected time and space to be with your child when they join your family. It is important to you, your child and your family that you take this leave. You will need to inform your employer or, if you're self-employed, to take steps to ensure you will be there for your child. This is a life-changing event and you will need to be with your child to ensure that they settle in with you and you start the process of bonding, giving it the best chance of success through your availability and proximity.

You will need to provide documentary evidence from your adoption agency that you are going through the adoption process. It will be of great help to your employers if you can give them information as early as possible in order for them to make appropriate arrangements to cover your absence. During the adoption process you can provide them with evidence from your adoption agency that you are going through this route to becoming a parent. Once you have been formally matched with a child then your adoption agency can provide you with a Matching Certificate.

Statutory Adoption Leave is generous and lasts for up to one year; indeed, your employer is likely to assume you will take your full entitlement. In order to qualify for this leave you must be adopting through an adoption agency properly recognised by UK law. You must also have completed at least 26 weeks' continuous employment with your organisation or company. Statutory Adoption Leave is split into Ordinary Adoption Leave (OAL), the first 26 weeks, and Additional Adoption Leave (AAL), the last 26 weeks. After the OAL you have the right to return to the same job. If you take AAL you have a right to return to the same job or, if that is not reasonably practicable, another suitable job. If you wish to change the date that you are going to return to work you have to give your employers at least eight weeks' notice. You can start this leave from the date of the placement of your child with you or from a fixed date up to two weeks before you expect this to happen. You should contact your HR department within seven days of being notified by your adoption agency that a match has been agreed. Tell them not only the date of being notified of the match but also when your child is likely to be placed with you, and when you will want to start your adoption leave.

It is worth staying in touch with your employer during your period of leave. Indeed, your employer has the legal right to maintain reasonable contact with you. Keeping in touch will remind them of your existence, and it will allow you to keep yourself up to speed with what is happening at work and start the process of deciding when you will return.

STATUTORY PATERNITY LEAVE

Statutory Paternity Leave can be taken by your partner, if applicable. As with Statutory Adoption Leave, it will be important to inform your employers as soon as possible of your intention to take this leave so they can make arrangements to cover your absence. You can take one week or two weeks but you can't take odd days off here and there. If you take two weeks, they have to be taken together. This leave can start on the day your child comes home with you or in the days or weeks following the placement but it has to be taken within eight weeks of the placement. In order to be eligible, just like Statutory Adoption Leave, you must have completed 26 weeks of uninterrupted employment up to the point when your adoption agency provides you with your Matching Certificate. Statutory Paternity Pay is also payable for this period.

OVERSEAS ADOPTIONS

These entitlements extend to overseas adoptions. The process is slightly more complicated in that the central authority involved in assessing and approving you as adoptive parents will provide the necessary documentation for your employers. Adoption or paternity leave can only be taken once the child has returned to the UK. As with adoptions in the UK it will be important to keep your employers up to date with what is happening.

Assessment is a joint endeavour, and knowing who and what you are dealing with will give you the strength and confidence to see this highly personal and emotional journey through to the end. At this point you should feel comfortable with the 'team' around you – both professionals and non-professionals – and be clear that they are there for you; a help, not a hindrance.

CHAPTER 4

Coming under Scrutiny

In society today, most of us are raised with a powerful sense of our own privacy; we are reassured that medical and financial records are confidential. When you are hoping to adopt, I'm afraid that you will have to accept a certain degree of intrusion into that private world. Scrutiny is an inevitable part of the adoption process. You will be required to open up your records to the authority handling your case so they can check you have the physical, mental and fiscal means to bring up a child. The assessment would be failing if it did not also help you to scrutinise yourself. While some of us are introspective, others are not. It is not in everyone's nature to examine their beliefs or motives in depth, particularly not in a public arena that is not therapeutic.

In this chapter, we will look at the areas of your life that will come under scrutiny during the assessment process. Additionally, there are some tips for preparing yourself for the process to minimise the amount of stress involved.

MEDICAL ASSESSMENT

How healthy you are plays an important part in meeting the basic requirements to adopt. It's common sense that the agencies want to ensure you are not going to pass away soon after a child is placed with you. They will want to reassure themselves that you have a good bit of life left in you. After all, the child you adopt will need you to be fit and well for at least the next 18 years or so. Of course no one can predict with certainty how long any of us is going to live but there are medical indicators that help paint a general picture.

In the light of this, both you and your partner, if you have one, will be required to have a medical assessment by your GP. Your GP's report and any specialist reports, if they are thought to be necessary, will be forwarded to the local authority or agency medical adviser. You will be expected to be honest about all matters relating to your health. The medical assessment involves examination of the health record your GP holds. Diseases and disorders that will interfere with your physical abilities to parent will be considered. There may, for example, be direct physical limitations on the sort of care you could provide for a child. This may have a bearing on the abilities of the child placed with you.

YOUR LIFESTYLE

The question of your 'habits' will come up – how much you drink, whether or not you smoke or take drugs and what sort of diet you have. All the little vices you indulge in will be examined from the perspective of whether they will affect your ability to look after a child or not. Changing attitudes to health mean that these matters are now taken very seriously indeed and may count against you. If you are a smoker, for instance, no agency will place a child under the age of five with you. If you need a reason to quit then this is it; pack in the fags and increase your chances of being approved for adoption.

ALCOHOL

Alcohol is another thorny issue. No one expects you to be teetotal but excessive drinking will make you unfit to parent. The key is to use your common sense. Alcohol is a pernicious problem and is associated with many difficulties in families including neglect, violence and other abuses. It might sound boring but moderation is the byword. A glass of wine with dinner isn't going to hurt anyone but if you down a bottle of wine on a regular basis then you might want to question yourself about whether you drink too much. People are often worried about the label of 'alcoholic' but it doesn't have to be that extreme for you to have a problem. We all know people who drink every day in varying amounts, dismissing it as just a way of un-winding. That may be the case but it will not mix well with parenting. Be honest about your consumption; this is something that can be dealt with if necessary. It may be that your drinking is a way of masking other problems that need sorting out. A level-headed approach to alcohol will also help you be a good role model for your child as they grow older and drinking becomes an issue. As for illegal drugs, they will not be tolerated in any degree.

HEALTHY EATING AND EXERCISE

These days there is a considerable focus on diet in the home. Your approach to food will be taken into account and examined. Chicken nuggets and chips on a daily basis would not provide the balanced diet a child needs. It may be that your social worker or agency will give you guidance on the sort of foods you should be offering your child. They may help you work out a weekly menu. Once again, a lot of it is using your common sense. Aim for the 'five a day' rule and you will be on the right road. You don't have to be fitness freaks but keeping an eye on healthy living through food and regular exercise is important. Children are unlikely to be placed with families who are morbidly obese as this is considered to be an unhealthy environment.

AGE

When you apply to adopt the question of how long you are likely to be around is brought into sharp focus. A factor in that is your age. There is no upper limit but the nearer you get to your pension the more concerned agencies will be. You might have a heart of gold and lots of love to give but if you are likely to die before your child grows up, you will be adding to your child's burden of loss. The sad truth is that the older you get the more likely you are to become ill and have less energy to deal with children.

Most agencies will have their protocols relating to age but generally they will want to ensure you have at least 20 years left in you. Remember, they are trying to place a child who may have had many separations and losses already, and they want to avoid that happening again as best they can. Obviously, the future cannot be predicted and there will always be unexpected serious health events but these will have to be dealt with as they occur. The agency will also look at any known medical conditions that you or your partner have.

MENTAL HEALTH

If you have suffered from a mental illness in the past it need not interfere with your approval to adopt, that is if the condition was mild, such as a period of low-grade depression, and has not recurred regularly. Local authorities differ but generally they will want you to have been symptom-free for at least three years. Mental disorders, like physical disorders, will require careful consideration, particularly where you have been under the care of a specialist. If you have a severe and enduring mental illness such as schizophrenia or manic-depressive psychosis you are unlikely to be accepted as an adoptive parent. The same applies if you have a history of alcohol or drug misuse.

These issues will be in your medical records which your GP holds and he or she is duty bound to inform the local authority or agency medical adviser about them. From the outset it is best to be honest about any history you may have of psychiatric problems and deal with it head on, rather than hoping it won't come up.

FINANCIAL STABILITY

You can't put a price on the joy a child will bring – a truism but only part of the picture. When it comes to adoption it is essential to address the question of how you intend to fund your new family member until they are old enough to support themselves. No one likes to place cold hard questions of finance alongside the incalculable emotional investment in a relationship with a child in need but you have to take off those rose-coloured spectacles and give this matter some serious consideration.

THE PRICE OF CHILDREN

Children in our western civilisation are not cheap. The cost of raising a family is always on the rise. It is tempting to put this issue to one side and simply say 'We'll manage somehow', as biological parents can do. While most biological parents seeking to start a family contemplate the financial ramifications of this, no one 'makes' them, unlike those seeking to adopt who have to provide evidence of their financial situation to outsiders.

There are regular news items about how much a child costs but it is hard to be accurate. Estimates by local authorities of how much it all comes to are worked out by taking into account numerous factors. They include the age of the child, any disability, their emotional or behavioural difficulties and whether or not they have been in trouble with the law. The fewer the problems the lower the sum.

The basic cost to the authority is thought to be over 12 times that of a child placed with parents – adoptive or biological. It is therefore not surprising that authorities are keen to get children out of care or foster homes. Clearly it is not just a desired social outcome but also a huge financial saving.

Since 2003, the Liverpool Victoria Insurance Group (LV) has undertaken an annual Cost of a Child Survey.[9] In 2007 it came up with a figure of £186,000 from birth to the age of 21. Included in this was university education. Well you might wince, but if you break it down it isn't so bad. It works out as roughly £9,000 a year or £700 a month or £20 a day. Cheap at the price you might say. It does get a bit more frightening if you include the cost of private education. For a day pupil add between £73,000 and £100,000 to the total, and most costly of all is boarding which puts another £130,000 on the final bill. That comes to a cool £250,000. These figures are not necessarily totally accurate as they differ from area to area. Remember, also, that they are spread over more than two decades.

The other consideration is the age of the child when you adopt. Adopting a child at the age of four, for example, means that you save at least £35,000! Liverpool Victoria considers university years as the most expensive at about £12,000 a year. The next most expensive bracket is between the ages of two and five, and the cheapest age range appears to be between 16 and 18 when some children presumably go out and get jobs. Furthermore, if you have a disabled child costs are about three times greater.

If having children was dependent on hard-nosed finances, the human race might be extinct by now. Adopting a child will be expensive whichever way you look at it, and sacrifices may have to be made. It may be that you are in a better position than biological parents as you will have time to do some financial planning and budgeting. Despite the number of zeros in evidence above you do not have to be rich to adopt. Far from it. There are various state benefits available, and whatever your financial position you will receive child benefit. You may be entitled to adoption pay, child trust fund allowance, and disability, mobility and carers' allowances. It is important to ensure you receive your full entitlement. Your social worker will advise you on how to go about making claims. Your tax position may also change so you might want to consult a financial adviser to ensure you do not pay any more than you need to. They will help you plan for your child's future in a tax-efficient way and deal with issues such as what happens when you die. How many of us intend to write our will but put the job at the bottom of the priority list so it never quite gets done?

You will need to demonstrate to the adoption agency that the way you manage your finances will not disadvantage a child placed with you. Therefore you will need to be open and realistic in appraising your current financial situation and how you use your money. Debt and the worries it engenders can be terribly corrosive to family unity and mental health.

FINANCIAL SUPPORT

As part of your adoption preparation your local authority is required to contemplate whether financial support should be paid to you, and inform you about what is available. Any decision they make should be given to you in written form and you should be able to make representations to them about your needs. They should review the financial support you require annually, and you are fully entitled to complain if you feel they have not assessed your needs fully or fairly. You are entitled to a needs assessment by your local authority any time after the Adoption Order, and your needs for financial support should be part of this. Your social worker should also be in a good position to advise you on any state benefits your family may be entitled to and how to obtain them (see page 104).

There is an expectation that court fees will be paid by your local authority if you are adopting from them. The fees currently range between £30 and £140. In some circumstances your local authority may help you with legal costs if the adoption is contested. You may be eligible for help with travel expenses during the matching phase. Your child may be entitled to similar expenses incurred in remaining in contact with their birth family. If your child has special needs you may be entitled to funds to help you buy special equipment or have your house adapted.

HOW TO PREPARE FOR MEETINGS WITH YOUR SOCIAL WORKER

Most of us get into a terrible sweat thinking about important meetings. Professionals will know, though, that the key to getting through them is preparation: going in with a plan. If you have thought it through you will feel and come across much more confident.

The meetings you have with your social worker will not be like any you have had before. You are not dealing with issues that relate to a workplace or business; this is as personal as it can get. You are concerned with making a family, taking on a child and giving them a safe home. So you start from quite a different place, one where emotions are accepted, even looked for. Being nervous is part of the picture. The social worker will know the ropes; they will have been through this dozens of times. You will be right to expect their understanding and encouragement from the moment you meet all the way through the adoption process and beyond.

It helps to consider what the meeting is about and what the social worker is looking for. As time goes by you will get to know them well enough to understand what they want to elicit from you or those close to you. From the word go your social worker will be looking for commitment. At the first meeting they will expect you to be quite clear, or at least have a good idea, about what you can offer and the sort of child you would like to adopt. This means you should have considered some of the basics such as the child's sex and age. Could you cope with disability? Is ethnicity, nationality or social background an issue? Do you envisage adopting again? Are there aspects of a child's make-up that you would find extremely difficult to manage, such as irritability, argumentativeness, faddy eating, anxiety or overactivity? These are all huge questions and are best considered and discussed with those closest to you in the days and weeks running up to your first meeting.

It is uncomfortable to put a child into categories or tick boxes about their qualities, treating them like an item on a shopping list or a computer matching service. It feels inhuman but it is the most expeditious way of getting this pairing right. If the child is old enough they are likely to have gone through the same considerations, and will have ticked boxes in order to find you. Although you need to have a clear idea of the sort of child you would like to adopt, a degree of flexibility is also important. Children don't come in tidy pre-packaged bundles.

Before the meeting, do some reading around adoption issues. You could, for instance, follow up any educational meetings you have attended and even start to look at publications that detail children looking for families. Consulting others about adoption – certainly your family but also those outside it, perhaps people who have prior experience – may give you some tips on what to expect.

You should not go to the first, and probably subsequent, meetings alone. I strongly recommend you take your partner or someone close, preferably a person who will be involved with your child. They will support you, make you feel stronger and hopefully be a good witness on your behalf. You may want to take more than one person along, which should be fine, but remember the social worker is looking at the potential parent or parents of the child, so although family and friends are important you are the one who is centre stage. Two pairs of eyes and ears are also useful. In the heat of the moment you may find that some of what was said has gone clean out of your mind. Nerves have a way of interfering with your memory. This is where your companion comes in handy. You will also be showing the social worker that you are not alone. They will want to see that you do have a strong support network around you.

Child-rearing is not something you can do properly in isolation.

The first meeting isn't an occasion for a sharp suit and a briefcase but do take a notebook and pen. You could also delegate, perhaps giving the job of taking down details to your partner or supporter. Easier still would be to bring a mini Dictaphone to record the session; this way you both can review what was said at your leisure. It will also enable you to concentrate on the interview rather than be distracted by trying to make a note of the ground you cover and what is said. You want to listen and engage as much as you can.

Looking through publications about adoption and reading documents will invariably prompt a number of questions you need answering. Write them down and bring them up at the meeting. The very fact you have done your own research will go down well with the social worker; it is a big tick in the 'commitment' box and shows you mean business. You should also get the answers you need.

As the assessment progresses it is important that you carry out the tasks you are given. This will not be an arbitrary bit of homework; there is a compulsory aspect to it. All applicants are asked to do the tasks and they are set for a reason. See this as part of the preparation for adoption and not as just a paper exercise.

Be open and honest in your answers, even when the questions sound a bit odd or silly. Join with the process; try to understand what the questions are about and don't be threatened by them. Without you a child who could have a family may be deprived of one; stick to your guns. Listen carefully and open your mind and self to what is happening. A pragmatic and can-do attitude will go down well with the social worker, particularly when based firmly in reality.

It is completely understandable if you find the prospect of this scrutiny unappealing and irksome, but there is a bright side. Experience shows that once you have examined these areas of your life with an outsider you are likely to have gained a much better grasp of where you stand both emotionally, physically and financially – always a useful exercise whether you are about to become a parent or not.

Now it is time to look at the assessment process in detail.

CHAPTER 5

The Assessment

Scrutiny is a scary matter for most people and now it's time to have a close look at what it's all about. Having someone rummage around in your personal affairs is not pleasant, but in adoption it is necessary. Think of it this way: if you were going to entrust a child to another person, wouldn't you want to go to the greatest of lengths to satisfy yourself that they were 100 per cent right for the job? As this chapter explains, the Assessment is the main tool used to establish your suitability. Remember, knowledge dispels fear, so take a deep breath, get a cup of tea, sit down in a comfy chair and read on.

Once your agency has agreed to take you on, the assessment begins in earnest. Assessment is at the core of the adoption process, so it is crucial that you get a feel for what it is all about. It is the way the agency or local authority gets the best placement it can for the children on its books. The centre of the adoption universe is the child. Supporting that are the statutory agencies that represent the child and have a legal duty to ensure their wellbeing. This is an enormous responsibility, and one that is generally discharged well. The agency or authority sees your role in all this as a means to realising that target. It wants to work with you just as much as you want to work with it, but before it can entrust you with its precious cargo it has to be as sure as is possible that you are right for the task. Therefore you go through a thorough examination over a period of months. The agency or authority isn't looking for 'perfect', just 'good-enough' parents.

You are required by law to undergo an assessment as to your suitability to become an adoptive parent. You will hear the terms 'assessment', 'Home Study' and 'Form F' used quite often – they are, in essence, one and the same thing. They come together to make up the file that the authority or agency has about your application. You will have to prove your worth to a number of people including your social worker, the adoption panel, the senior officer of the adoption agency, your child's social worker, your child and you. This process can be wearing but will stand you in good stead; as an adoptive parent you'll be repeating the process on a daily basis with your child or children, becoming that parent who is 'good enough'.

Assessments are moving towards looking at competency-based values (for example, what strengths and abilities you have to manage real-life situations as opposed to, say, your educational level or financial situation). It is a very fair, upfront and clear way of being able to ascertain what individuals are 'really' able to achieve. How you handle yourself is therefore important, especially in the context of the trials and tribulations of daily life. It should be possible to reveal to your social worker information about your ways of thinking, acting and being without necessarily articulating them as such. This can be achieved by describing various experiences in your life and how you have coped with them. Sharing your past experiences in this way is subtle and effective. The social worker will be in your home so make them welcome. You could sit them down with a cup of tea and chat in a relaxed atmosphere about events you feel have made you who you are. The same scenario works for others in the house, such as your partner or other children if you have them.

The questions you will be asked are standard. They will be put to everyone applying to become an adoptive parent. Many will be quite straightforward and direct; some may seem desperately intrusive; others quite pointless. These will not be questions that have a yes or no answer, nor will there be a right or wrong response. This is not an exam; it is a way of getting to know you in more depth. The whole process is really designed to try and understand how you think and how this will relate to your child. The way you answer the questions and justify yourself is likely to be as important as the content of your answers. Try and bear in mind that the questions are asked for a reason and are part of a legal process. Your social worker is just discharging their duty and liability to children for whom they are responsible. It is not personal but it is important.

The assessment can only really look at how you are now. Obviously, there are records of your past and expectations of your future; but using either of these as a guide to how you will be as a parent for an adoptive child has limitations. At least with the past there is something concrete to go on, but no one can see into the future with certainty. Those assessing you have a difficult task because their judgements about how you will be in the future have to be made on who you are now, the person standing before them. They will have to use their experience and instincts to get into your head, to get a feel for how you function, your personality, views, strengths and weaknesses. It is a huge task but it is considered the best way of establishing whether or not you will be right for adoption.

You may feel a bit anxious that you have limited experience, especially with children. Don't worry. Part of what your social worker is doing is weighing up your potential. They will be assessing how you will be when it comes to future learning and development; how you will cope with the myriad issues life can throw up. In order to do this they need to get to know you, to get a feel for your attributes. This assessment is not about just your abilities but also those of the people around you, the family and/or friends who will form part of the home structure for the child. Stock up on your coffee and tea supplies and prepare to do a lot of talking!

Another good tip is to brace yourself for some odd questions. For example, your social worker might pop in a question about how you would cope if the child announced at some future date that they were gay or lesbian, or what you would do if they started shoplifting. Try not to choke on your rich tea biscuit; they are only doing their job. These kinds of question are not indiscriminate prying; they are carefully placed within the process and have a clear purpose. How you answer them gives a clue to your coping mechanisms but there is also a bit of a shock tactic coming into play as the questions make you take a close look at the possible realities of what you are undertaking. The aim is to provide you with food for thought so both you and your social worker can start to tease out your thinking processes and the beliefs underpinning them. The questions also serve as a measure of your resolve and, if you mean business, they are unlikely to deter you.

THE HOME STUDY

The Home Study is just that: a study (of you and yours) that takes place in your home, not in some impersonal office or clinic somewhere. Your social worker comes to your home and works through the formal assessment with you. It is a collaboration between you, your family and your social worker, a joint effort in which self-assessment is as important as the assessment of you by the social worker. It will explore your motivations and personal history. Both you and your social worker will want to be assured that the adoption of a child is the right thing for you and your family and that, as far as the assessment goes, you are suited to become an adoptive parent. The study will build up a picture of not only you but also the environment in which you live and can provide for a child. It will help the social worker to get a better understanding of the type of child or children that you would be best suited to adopt.

The Home Study takes between six and eight months. It involves at least half a dozen in-depth interviews with you. Social workers will also speak to members of your family unit, both with you present and on their own. While the study is taking place, you will also be given further information about the adoption process. This might take the form of private study but is more usually in the form of adoption preparation classes (see pages 33–37). You will also be 'set' homework in order to look at and be able to discuss important issues related to your child, parenting and beliefs.

The Home Study is a chance to add to your knowledge of the important issues involved in adoption, such as:

➤ your child's educational needs
➤ the importance of heritage in the development of identity
➤ separation and loss
➤ how deprivations in your child's life before joining you are likely to manifest, and how you might start to understand and manage them

You will explore how bonding and attachment work and how they can be disrupted by your child's experience of neglect and abuse. You will find out what resources are available to help you and your child after adoption is completed.

It is up to your social worker to make the Home Study as comfortable and open as possible. People tend to feel they are likely to be judged by some 'perfect parent' standard. This is not so. Perfect parents don't exist. Good-enough parents do, and that is what the Home Study is all about – trying to assess if you will be 'good-enough' parent(s).

'GOOD-ENOUGH' PARENTS

The British psychoanalyst D.W. Winnicott introduced the world to the concept of 'good-enough' parenting as opposed to 'perfect parenting' where all the child's needs are met all of the time. His view was that holding on to a child and perpetually meeting every need at all times would in fact be harmful as it would not allow them to develop. In order for a child to develop normally, he argued, they need a gradual separation from their mother; hence she was not perfect but 'good enough'. This term is used widely today to reassure people that doing their best as parents is all that can realistically be expected or desired from them. It is likely you will hear the term time and again as you go through the adoption process. (For more on being a 'good-enough' parent, see Chapter 10.)

During the Home Study you might feel you are on trial. That is not unreasonable because, in effect, you are – not in a court of law but in your own home. An outsider has come in – at your invitation, remember – and is rummaging around in your personal affairs. You may feel they are peering into dark corners, if there are any, and possibly trying to trip you up or uncover something long hidden. It is at this point you may come up against a realisation that there is a distinct imbalance in the power structure of this process. There is no doubt that the social worker and the agency are in control. They have the power – not God-like but not far off – as their views will either help or hinder your future as an adoptive parent in a major way. The feelings or beliefs engendered by this imbalance may be reinforced by issues of culture, religion, class, gender, sexual orientation, marital status, ethnicity, language and so on. It behoves all social workers to acknowledge and address issues relating to this disparity in power and to ensure equity, understanding, openness, fairness and transparency in all their dealings with you.

Never lose sight of the fact that you are the one who chose to make this happen. There is no gain without pain, as the exercise gurus say, and in this instance we are dealing with much more important issues than a few toned muscles. The pain is to be under close scrutiny for a relatively short but intense period of time; the gain is to realise your passionate wish to have a family. Although the power of the adoption agencies is rooted in law, remember that you also have power. Without you there would be no adoption, no home and no family or long-term care for a disadvantaged child or children. We must not forget the professional and personal satisfaction social workers gain from knowing they have played a part in providing a child with a loving family.

Adoption is about committing yourself to another person for life. It is not an easy option and you must take this path fully secure in the knowledge of its benefits and difficulties. Pregnancy has a nine-month gestation, which is just a bit longer than the time the Home Study takes. However, the study is a more thorough preparation for parenthood than the majority of birth parents receive. Your ability to commit fully will form part of the Home Study. To approach adoption half-heartedly is a big mistake. If you lack commitment this will ring alarm bells with your social worker. Then again, initial impressions can change. Assessment will allow you to build up a relationship with your social worker which will provide context and emotional background to the questions they need to ask.

HONESTY – THE BEST POLICY

All adults involved in the adoption process are advised to be as honest as possible at every step of the way. Honesty and trust work together. As a parent you have to be a good role model; part of that will involve you being as honest as you can with your children. This is especially true for an adopted child who is likely to have been let down many times in their life before coming to you. Trust is earned through behaviours that match words. You will need to be understanding and tolerant of children who take time to reveal their feelings honestly, particularly their vulnerabilities. Generally, they will express their difficulties through behaviours, some more difficult than others.

Lies have a way of being exposed sooner or later. In themselves they might not seem important but they will crush the trust you have built up with your social worker and the agency. If they distrust you at this point, why would they decide to trust you enough to place a child with you in the future? Consider what the lie is about. Is it really worth jeopardising your family for? There is little that can shock the agency team who will have come across most of life's grubby extremes.

By the same token it is right that you should expect complete honesty from adoption agency staff. You must receive at least as much honesty from social workers as they expect from you. You are vitally important in the process – indeed key – even though you may not feel this at times. Good social workers will ensure you have a relationship based on trust; they will put a high value on honesty, both giving and receiving.

Honesty is obviously a must in your relationship with your child. However, honesty delivered in a blunt, inconsiderate way can be brutal and appear uncaring. Sensitivity is essential in dealing with your child. Think it through. It is not what you say but how and when you say it that matters, particularly when talking about your child's past. Empathic listening, putting yourself in your child's shoes, understanding and warmth will help you build the right environment in which trust and honesty can grow between you. It is not a failing to seek help on how best to impart or discuss difficult facts. The way you deal with it will assist or hamper the way your child manages such issues in their life.

THE PROSPECTIVE ADOPTERS' REPORT OR FORM F

You will become quite familiar with this form. It is a template for you and your social worker to provide the information required by an adoption panel in order to decide whether you are, in their opinion, suitable to become an adoptive parent. Not surprisingly, you might find Form F a rather daunting prospect. Don't be put off. Your social worker will have filled it in many times and is there to help you. They will provide you with an overview to get started and explain the rationale behind the questions, their depth and relevance. This will help you understand the type of questions you will have to answer. It will also help you to deal with some of the emotions they will engender from time to time. For example, a degree of indignation, even outright anger or hostility, may be triggered by questions that seem irrelevant, intrusive, politically correct or even downright stupid. These feelings may be enhanced by the fact that biological parents don't have to go through this process.

At times like this it's important to take a step back and get things into perspective. All of the questions relate to the need to provide a disadvantaged child with a safe family and are based on years of study and research in this field. If you feel negatively towards aspects of Form F don't take it out on the social worker. They are just the messenger; they did not compile the form. If you wish to adopt it is up to you to furnish the evidence to those whose legal duty it is to protect the child. Form F requires a joint effort. All parties need to play their part to persuade the statutory authorities that, as far as can be ascertained from the information obtained, you will be a safe and committed parent through both the good times and bad. Look at this process as a test of endurance, a hurdle to be overcome, rather than a criticism or personal slight.

Used correctly, Form F is an extremely useful template for collating information. The questions posed by the form require in-depth thought and you are likely to need time to think about your responses; it is not a tick-box exercise. The process should be one of open and frank discussion, as well as detailed exploration of motivations, opinions, beliefs and evidence. If your social worker seems to be slavishly following Form F, and you feel you are not being treated as an individual, you should discuss this with them. A rigid approach is unlikely to be helpful. It may lead to conflict between you or encourage you to provide what you perceive as the 'correct' answers to get the whole thing over as favourably and quickly as possible. Such a situation would be particularly alarming for people who have already been through much heart-searching and difficulty on their journey from childlessness to adoption.

Occasionally mistakes will be made. Perhaps you feel you are not being heard or there is a disagreement of some kind. You might feel dislike or even anger towards the social worker at times. Ideally, any problems should be dealt with in a spirit of openness by all parties; this hiccup may even improve your relationship if handled well. If you continue to have problems, however, then it is wise to sound the alarm. Once again, be open about it. Talk it through with your social worker. If that doesn't help, raise any issues with a more senior team member at the agency. You must feel that the agency is not only truly on your side but also honest and straightforward in its dealings with you. Your relationship should be one of mutual benefit.

WHAT YOUR SOCIAL WORKER NEEDS TO KNOW

THE PEOPLE IN YOUR LIFE

Relationships are a key area for scrutiny during the assessment. The condition of your relationships will be examined in more detail than you would normally expect to share with an outsider. It sounds intrusive but, oddly enough, many individuals find this process particularly useful. Having to sit down and review how you get on with those around you, what you feel about them and how you function on a day-to-day basis or in a crisis can lead to greater understanding of your relationships and provide an affirmation of your feelings. As a beneficial side-effect, this process can refresh and reinvigorate your relationships, particularly if you have been through the trials and tribulations of childlessness and fertility treatment. This is enhanced by an open and honest relationship with your social worker. Being open to this area of investigation will give them the message that you are flexible and able to accept advice, help and change.

Adoption is not something you do in isolation – far from it. The whole process is essentially about relationships, often complex ones that must be nurtured and dealt with sensitively. You will develop a whole raft of new relationships; most importantly with your child or children, their carers and possibly members of their family, perhaps even their biological parent(s). Long before the child comes into the picture, though, you will be getting to know your social worker, other adoptive parents and health professionals. From the very first stages of the adoption process, how you get on with all the people involved is relevant; it will be regarded as an indicator of how you will cope as an adoptive parent. This is not to say you have to be the life and soul of the party, gregarious to the extent of becoming irritating. It is much more subtle than that. You do not have to 'perform' for these new people in your life. The wisest course of action is to be yourself – honesty is the best policy – but it will pay dividends to be aware that your behaviour is seen as a powerful predictive tool.

If you are a quiet, loving person, that will come across just as well as someone who bounces around hugging everyone. Remember, the agency team will be trying to establish how you will be with your adoptive child, and with a child comes a considerable number of new faces. Think about it – there will be schooling, social groups, old and new friends/family, medical or social needs carers. It's a long list. The agency team has to make a prediction based on how you are at this point in your life. It's a tough call and getting to know you as well as they can gives them their best chance of getting it right. Their experience will guide them.

ALL ABOUT YOU

The assessment will require you to tell your story from the outset and to explain what sort of childhood you had. All areas of your past and present will be put under the spotlight. It can feel quite threatening and daunting at times but also revelatory and empowering at others. The fear of not being accepted may cast a shadow over your thoughts. Don't worry – this is only natural. Stay committed, determined, truthful and honest. It is that frame of mind which will help you succeed.

The Home Study will set out to explore your views – and what has informed them – on things such as:

➤ social and personal identity
➤ roles and relationships
➤ child-rearing and development
➤ ethnicity
➤ education

You will explore what motivates you, what your expectations are and how closely these tie in with the reality of adoption today. You will learn:

- about yourself
- how open you are to seeking new information
- how you incorporate new learning into your views
- how you adjust to new information
- how open you are to change

The Home Study is an opportunity to explore:

- how flexible you, your family and social circle are in your interactions
- your beliefs about normal mental and physical health and how to keep your child healthy and safe
- the importance of social support and your support network
- your attitudes to problems and abilities to solve them
- your strengths
- issues from your past such as grief, bereavement and managing loss

Your adoption agency will want to be as sure as possible that you are going to provide a safe and loving home and family for your child. Although reading the future is an imprecise art, the best clues originate in the past. Therefore, in order to give yourself the best chance of success, choose referees who have known you the longest, preferably since childhood. Some agencies will want to talk to up to half a dozen referees, obtaining references from three of them. Unless your referees agree, you will not see their references.

SPECIFIC QUALITIES

Adoption means allowing another person into your life. Your capacity to integrate is therefore high on your social worker's agenda. Your family and social group should be able to provide the safety, security and continuity to allow children to integrate their past into the present. You will be dealing with children who may have had difficult, painful experiences and complicated relationships. Other desirable qualities in adoptive parents include:

➤ open and flexible attitudes
➤ an ability to face up to and endure sadness and loss in others without being overwhelmed or embarrassed
➤ a natural tendency to put the needs of children first and to understand and not be threatened or undermined by your children's previous relationships
➤ families who can honestly examine and acknowledge their strengths and weaknesses and who are big enough to seek and use help when it is needed
➤ perseverance and determination – it is important to be able to model security and safety to your child, especially as so many adoptive children have been let down so badly in the past

The addition of a child to a family changes that child and family forever. Any emotional pain or difficulties your child is going through will affect you and other members of your family. During the assessment an attempt will therefore be made to make you more aware of your own family history and how you and your family currently function – how you communicate, resolve conflicts, praise each other, share things that matter. Your natural coping strategies develop over the years and are the result of learning as you go through life. Build on the skills and strengths you have.

From the agency's point of view, it is of the utmost importance that you are tenacious, that you will stick with your child through thick and thin; that when they are distressed you will provide an anchor – both emotional and physical – for them to hang on to. Giving these children a solid base, a home ground they can trust, is the goal of everyone involved. Part of the assessment is to encourage you to examine closely whether or not you have what it takes to create a secure world for a child, to help you look inside and get an understanding of how you tick. After all, the better you know yourself the more able you will be to give that self to another person. You have to believe in yourself. Having external confirmation that you can do it will make you even stronger and feed that ability.

Agencies are also looking for a flexible approach and an open mind. They want someone who can learn about what lies behind the difficulties a child has had to date, how they came to behave in certain ways and how to manage that behaviour. No one knows it all; you must be willing to listen to and learn from the experience of others. Being pig-headed and insisting that you know best will not be the solution to problems that crop up.

Communication is fundamental to all relationships, none more so than with the child who is placed in your care. The aim is to hear them and allow them to feel that they are being heard. By the same token, you must know how to get your message across to them. Communication can be complex; 90 per cent of communication is non-verbal. An awareness of what is being said without speaking will help you to understand your child better, to interpret how they are feeling and possibly to intercept any difficult behaviour before it erupts into a full-blown crisis. It is worth asking your social worker or other professionals you come across in this process about how you can pick up the wordless signals from your child. Your interest will be noted, as will your awareness of the importance of communication.

The agency will want to see that you can communicate well, that you are prepared to listen, respond and act on advice from them. As the child's champion, you may at times have to engage and communicate with statutory bodies, such as local authorities, health and educational organisations and the courts, in order access services available to you and your adoptive child.

YOUR PROFILE

The preferred profile for an adoptive parent is someone who is clear about wanting to adopt and the reasons for coming to this decision. They will be resilient, determined and relaxed in the face of a crisis. They are likely to enjoy challenge; they will be child-centred and able to step back to view problems dispassionately while remaining emotionally available and involved with their children. They are also likely to be a good communicator, even down to being comfortable with – possibly sympathetic to – the child's birth parents. They must be realistic and understand the importance of time and stability. Part of that realism is to know that sometimes love is not enough; you need to have skills that go beyond a hug. Cuddling is wonderful, but in the world of relationships things are much more complicated than giving someone a hug. If you don't know that then prepare to learn. Like most things in life, all this is not cast in stone. If you are reading this and thinking you don't tick all the boxes, do not despair. The phrase 'preferred profile' is telling; the assessment procedure is flexible, just as you will be. If bits of the profile are missing, that need not be the end of your chances; it is up to the social worker who gets to know you to decide what is important and relevant regarding your personal attributes at the end of the day. For instance, you may feel you are useless at communicating with children but your social worker will spot the fact that once you are a parent you will quickly get the hang of it. After all, no one examines biological parents so closely, and generally that works out okay.

LOOKING WITHIN

It is quite natural for you to feel anxious and apprehensive about the assessment. Most of us have become used to talking about our problems and weaknesses with professionals such as doctors, but the assessment is different. What is at stake is the future of a family you want to build. This will be a unique experience, one that involves an in-depth scrutiny of you and your life. Odd as it may seem, close examination of our vulnerabilities may give clues as to how best to move forwards. So often we can let our limitations or vulnerabilities drag us down or hold us back. The human spirit is about overcoming adversity. Adoption is about overcoming the fact that your child is not biologically yours, loving them and taking them into your own family.

The Home Study should help and encourage you to recognise your strengths, many of which you may have played down or ignored or were even unaware of. This is not a mantra for positive thinking but rather a nudge in the direction of taking a fresh look at yourself and challenging how you see your capabilities. In my experience we are generally more resourceful and skilful than we may lead ourselves to believe. Once you acknowledge that you may be hiding lights under bushels then you can get on with the business of accepting what you are good at, working on the bits that aren't up to scratch and consigning the bits you cannot change to a mental scrapheap.

This is not the time to be coy about what you can and cannot do. You will need all your resources mustered when it comes to parenting, so take advantage of this assessment process as it can help you see yourself much more clearly. Don't regard the social worker or agency as the enemy – they are in place for you and your child to help you negotiate the journey. They are on your side and want you to succeed and to see your new family thrive. Getting a better grasp of your inner mechanics is one way of helping that to happen.

Just as authorities recognise the existence of stereotypes, it will be important that you admit and manage your stereotypes of social workers and statutory bodies. Acknowledgement is the first step towards change and avoidance of bias. Once you have managed to be honest about your preconceptions of the professionals you will encounter, you can get on with the business in hand. In all likelihood you will discover that your preconceived ideas about these people were well wide of the mark.

The process of assessment will provide the really important in-depth information to enable the adoption panel to consider your case and recommend your acceptance or not. They may recommend deferral while further information is sought, though this is uncommon. You will hopefully have attended the adoption panel hearing and will have got a feeling of how things are going. The final decision rests with the senior officer in your agency who will be keen to let you know his or her decision as soon as possible. Whether you are successful or not you will be informed in writing and possibly also verbally by your social worker.

There is no doubt that assessment is a challenge. What helps is that it is a clearly defined process based on precedent, paperwork and people who know what they are doing. It is a concerted enterprise seeking to find out what makes you tick and weigh up your family's capacity to provide a stable base and the emotional affection, basic care and security required for your child to develop to their full intellectual, emotional and physical potential.

PART THREE:

FINDING YOUR CHILD

CHAPTER 6

Your Child and the Adoption Process

In the following chapters we look at perhaps the most difficult and yet most rewarding step in adoption – choosing your child. It is possible that up until now most of your thoughts about becoming a parent have involved a 'fantasy child', a mental image of the little one of your dreams. There is nothing wrong with that: it is quite normal to have your own idea of the child you want. There is a 'but', though. In the real world these children come with their own history and the fantasy is unlikely to fit the flesh-and-blood reality.

At the heart of the adoption process are children who need a home, a family, someone to love and care for them. You will no doubt wonder about the road that brought them to this sorry state at such a tender age. Of course there is room to romanticise – the picture of Oliver Twist looms large – but this is the real world. To do the best for your new family member you have to tackle life armed with facts and not fancies. You are the turning point for this child; you will be expected to meet their needs and champion their cause just like any other parent. You can become stronger in this endeavour by knowing what to expect. Indeed, you have a need and a right to learn as much as you can about the child you are offered. The more you know about their background the better able you will be to help deal with any physical and emotional fallout. Preparation is all.

The upper age limit for a child being put up for adoption is 18. As you might expect, it is rare for someone to be adopted once they get into their late teens. The children who need adoption come in all shapes and sizes, from infants and toddlers to adolescents. Some will be in family groups of two or more who want to be adopted together. Some will have physical or mental disabilities. Others will come from a variety of ethnic groups. Many will have had a difficult start to life. Some will be struggling to cope with the trauma they have been through; others will appear to be fine but their true state of mind will come to light later on. Others will really be fine; they will have dealt with their experiences and be ready to move on. Your job, with the help of the professionals, is to identify the trouble spots and know how to deal with them. Anticipating the troubles you might encounter will be a great help.

PLACING A CHILD FOR ADOPTION

Children are put up for adoption only after extensive efforts have been made to keep them with their birth families. The accepted view is that it is in the best interests of the child for them to remain with their biological family if at all possible. This is not always the case, however, particularly when the evidence is clear that the birth parents or family cannot meet the physical, emotional and developmental needs of the child, especially if the child is thought to be at risk.

The child that comes to you is likely to have been 'looked after'. This term, used by the professionals, means the child has either been fostered or spent time in a community home. This happens while the authorities try to reunite them with their family. The local authority and adoption agency will have considered a number of options for the child including long-term fostering, a Residence Order or Special Guardianship Order (see page 68). Any of these will be used if it is thought the child will benefit from a continued link with their natural family or if they are older and do not wish to be adopted.

PLACEMENT BY CONSENT

Placement by consent is where a parent or guardian is prepared, freely and unconditionally, to consent to the placement of their child for future adoption. The consent of a mother who has just given birth will not be valid if given within the first six weeks of the birth. Therefore, a child placed with an adoption agency under the age of six weeks will have to be looked after by the authority until they are six weeks old. At this time the local authority can ask for parental consent for placement or apply for a Placement Order (see overleaf). This consent can be withdrawn at any time until an Adoption Order is made. The consent must be given on a special form and, in England, witnessed by an officer (the reporting officer) from CAFCASS (the Children and Family Courts Advisory and Support Services).

PLACEMENT ORDERS

A Placement Order authorises a local authority to place a child for adoption where there is no parental consent, or where consent should be dispensed with. The consent of a parent or guardian may not be necessary if:

(a) the parent or guardian cannot be found or they are incapable of giving their agreement because, for instance, they are mentally ill

(b) the court is satisfied that the welfare of the child requires that consent be dispensed with

The welfare of the child outweighs the rights of the birth parents. However, the courts must still consider the impact on the child of ceasing to be a member of their birth family and the change in their relationship with the family that adoption would bring. Local authorities must apply for a Placement Order (which enables a local authority to place a child with prospective adopters) if a child is the subject of a Care Order (which grants parental responsibility to a local authority) and there is no parental consent, or if they consider the child to be at risk of significant harm. A court cannot make a Placement Order unless an effort has been made to notify the people who have parental responsibility for the child that an application is being made.

CONTESTED CASES

Where children are placed for adoption against their parents' wishes, these are called contested cases. The uncertainty can be very stressful for adoptive parents. If your child's case is contested by their birth parents, it is important to seek legal advice. Even though a child has been placed with you there is no certainty until the Adoption Order is made. Indeed, the scrutiny continues after a child is placed with you. Your social worker is legally required to visit you weekly for the first month, and subsequently at three months after the last visit and then every six months until an Adoption Order is granted. The aim of these reviews is not only to see how the child is developing but also to get a feel for when or if the child feels ready to be assimilated and adopted into your family. Only after the Adoption Order is your child legally yours. It is worth remembering that even after the Adoption Order your relationship with the local authority may continue on and off for years.

INFORMATION ABOUT YOUR CHILD

All agencies have to create a case record of each child. It's like a 'This is Your Life – so far' dossier that should answer a lot of questions you will have about a child. You will not be allowed to see it until you have been approved. Once you are through that crucial hurdle the social worker will come up with a possible match, send you this document for you to study and then suggest a meeting to discuss a placement. From this, you should be able to get a good idea if you want to proceed; any doubts you may have should be discussed with your social worker. If you remain in doubt, do not proceed. Think of how this might affect the child.

YOUR CHILD'S ADOPTION CASE RECORD

An adoption agency has a legal requirement to open a case file on those children in its care for whom adoption is felt to be in their best interests. This record is known as the child's adoption case record and amongst other administrative documents it should contain:

➤ the child's original birth certificate and birth details (time, weight, type of delivery etc)

➤ description and details (including family tree) of the birth family and household, and any other relevant documents especially if a child's needs are thought to be complex or high

➤ photographs, certificates, other significant personal mementos and Life Story book/disc

➤ medical information provided by birth parents

➤ details of the child's development assessment

➤ the Child's Permanence Report

➤ Adoption Placement Report, Adoption Support Plan and other documents prepared and presented for the Adoption Panel

➤ record of social work with child about adoption, including recording of direct work

➤ etails of siblings, together with any assessments and decisions to place brothers and sisters separately, including minutes of relevant meetings

➤ all relevant Adoption Panel and adoption agency decision maker's documentation

➤ details of all reviews undertaken on a child before and after adoption was identified as the best option for the child

➤ assessments, correspondence and signed agreements relating to post-placement and post-adoption contact

➤ any other key correspondence to and from members of the child's birth family

➤ list and copies of information supplied to child and adopters

➤ Later Life letter/information from the birth parents to the child and the social worker outlining the circumstances of the adoption plan

➤ the Adoption Placement Plan with any amendments and social work reports to a child after placement including any Adoption Reviews

➤ court reports and other documents

➤ a copy of the applicable Care Order; Placement Order; Adoption Order etc

➤ any recording relating to birth records, counselling of the adopted person or requests for access to the Adoption Case Record

➤ any veto – absolute or qualified – registered by the adopted person after they attain 18 years

The adoption agency is required – as far as reasonably practicable – to provide a counselling service for the child. They must explain the adoption procedure to the child in an appropriate manner, including the legal implications, and provide relevant written information. They are obliged to find out the child's wishes and feelings regarding possible placement for adoption with a new family, their religious and cultural upbringing and contact with parents or guardians or other relatives.

The adoption agency must also provide a counselling service for the parent or guardian of the child and explain the adoption procedure to them. It must explain and provide written information about the legal implications of:

➤ giving consent to placement for adoption
➤ giving consent to the making of a future Adoption Order
➤ a Placement Order
➤ adoption

The agency is also required to ascertain the wishes and feelings of the parent or guardian and any other person the agency considers relevant regarding the child and its placement for adoption (this applies to fathers even where the father of the child does not have parental responsibility). It needs to consider any wishes and feelings about the child's religious and cultural upbringing as well as contact if the child is placed for adoption.

The child's case record will contain basic information, such as their name, sex, date and place of birth, local authority area and address. A physical description of them and a photograph will be included. Their nationality should be recorded as well as their racial origin, cultural and linguistic background and religious persuasion, including details of any baptism, confirmation or equivalent ceremonies. Necessary legal information includes:

(a) whether the child is looked after or is provided with accommodation under section 59(1) of the 1989 Act
(b) details of any order made by a court with respect to

the child under the 1989 Act including the name of the court, the order made and the date on which the order was made

(c) whether the child has any rights to, or interest in, property or any claim to damages under the Fatal Accidents Act 1976 or otherwise which he or she stands to retain or lose if he or she is adopted

There will be an account of the child's life in care since birth and a description of the child's personality; their social, emotional and behavioural development; their interests, likes and dislikes. Any difficulties the child may have with activities of daily life such as feeding, washing and dressing themselves must also be recorded. The child's educational history will include:

(a) the names, addresses and types of nurseries or schools attended with dates

(b) a summary of their progress and attainments

(c) whether they are subject to a statement of special educational needs under the Education Act 1996

(d) any special needs they have in relation to learning

(e) where they are looked after, details of their personal education plan prepared by the local authority

Information will be recorded about the child's relationship with their parent or guardian, any brothers or sisters and other relatives they may have and, in addition, any other person the agency considers relevant. An assessment will be made of the value of each relationship to the child and a decision made as to whether it should continue or not. There will also be a note of the ability and willingness of the child's parent or guardian, or any other person the agency considers relevant, to provide the child with a secure environment in which he or she can develop, and otherwise to meet his or her needs. A description will be given of the current arrangements for, and the type of contact between, the child and the child's parent or guardian or other person with parental responsibility for him or her, as well as his or her father, any relative, friend or other person. The child's case record should also include any other relevant information which might assist the adoption panel and the adoption agency.

YOUR CHILD'S HEALTH REPORT

It is essential that you have full access to your child's health record. Unless the adoption agency's doctor advises against it, the agency must make arrangements for the child to be examined by a registered medical practitioner and obtain a report on the child's health. This will include any treatment the child is receiving and their need for any ongoing or future health care. The agency should also make arrangements for any other medical or psychiatric examination or tests recommended by their medical adviser. Written reports will be required for all of these. Such examinations or tests may be refused by a child who has sufficient understanding to make an informed decision on the matter. This may mean that you will have less information about your child's health. The adoption agency must also obtain, as far as reasonably practicable, information about the health of each of the child's natural parents and his brothers and sisters (including any half-siblings).

Your child's health report should include the following information:

1. Name, date of birth, sex, weight and height.
2. A neonatal (from birth to one month) report on the child, including:
   a. details of their birth and any complications
   b. the results of a physical examination and screening tests
   c. details of any treatment given
   d. details of any problem in management and feeding
   e. any other relevant information which may assist the adoption panel and the adoption agency
   f. the name and address of any registered medical practitioner who may be able to provide further information about any of the above matters
3. A full health history of the child, including:
   a. details of any serious illness, disability, accident, hospital admission or attendance at an outpatient department, and in each case any treatment given
   b. details and dates of immunisations
   c. a physical and developmental assessment according to age, including an assessment of vision and hearing and of neurological, speech and language development and any evidence of emotional disorder
   d. for a child over five years of age, the school health history (if available)
   e. details of how the child's physical and mental health and medical history have affected their physical, intellectual, emotional, social or behavioural development
4. Any other relevant information which may assist the adoption panel and the adoption agency.

YOUR CHILD'S BIOLOGICAL FAMILY

The adoption agency should have information about the child's birth parents, including their names, sex, date and place of birth and local authority area and address, and if possible a photograph or a physical description. Their nationality, racial origin, cultural and linguistic backgrounds and religious persuasion are also important. Information about children's other relatives or any other person the agency considers relevant should be recorded. Remember, this information will help you form an overview of your child's origins and how they came into your family.

Similar information should be available about your child's brothers and sisters. If they are under 18, there should be details of:

➤ where and with whom they are living
➤ whether they are looked after or provided with accommodation by the local authority
➤ details of any court order made with respect to them under the 1989 Act, including the name of the court, the order made and the date on which the order was made
➤ whether they are also being considered for adoption

A family history should be pieced together and include details such as whether the child's parents were married to each other at the time of the child's birth (or have subsequently married), and if so, the date and place of marriage and whether they are divorced or separated. If the child's parents are not married it's important to know whether the father has parental responsibility for the child and, if so, how it was acquired. The report should contain any information about steps that may or may not have been taken to establish paternity if the identity of the child's father is unknown; likewise, any attempts – successful or otherwise – made to locate the child's father. Details of previous marriages or civil partnerships the child's parents have had should be noted. As far as possible, a family tree should be drawn with details of the child's relations, including as much information as possible. If it is practicable, the life story of each of the child's parents should be obtained, as this will be helpful for the child later on. This could include details of how the child's parents experienced being parented, and how that influenced them and their relationships with their partner/partners and the child. It's important to build up a picture of the child's wider family and their role in relation to the child's parents and any of the child's brothers or sisters.

THE PERMANENCE REPORT

Your child's permanence report is a written statement that contains the following information:

1. Specified information about your child and their family.
2. A summary, written by the agency's medical adviser, of the state of your child's health, their health history and any need for care that might arise in future.
3. The wishes and feelings of your child regarding placement for adoption, adoption and contact with parents, guardians or other important individuals.

4. The wishes and feelings of your child's parent or guardian, which may include the father or any other person the agency considers relevant, regarding placement, adoption and contact.

5. The views of the agency about your child's need for contact with their parent or guardian or other relative or with any other person the agency considers relevant, and the arrangements the agency proposes to make for allowing any person to have contact with your child.

6. An assessment of your child's social, emotional and behavioural development and any related needs.

7. An assessment of the parenting capacity of your child's parent or guardian (this may include the father).

8. A chronology of the decisions or actions taken by the adoption agency regarding your child.

9. An analysis of the options for the future care of your child which have been considered by the agency and why placement for adoption is considered the preferred option for your child.

10. Any other information the agency considers relevant.

(Adoption Agency Regulations 2005 © Crown Copyright)

The child's permanence report is forwarded to the adoption panel along with their health report and information on the health of each of the child's parents. You will receive a copy of your child's permanence report. The adoption panel will then consider the child's case and make a recommendation to the agency as to whether the child should be placed for adoption. It may request further information and, where appropriate, obtain legal advice. The panel has a duty to consider giving advice to the adoption agency about the arrangement proposed for allowing individuals contact with the child and whether or not the authority should apply for a Placement Order in respect of this child. If their whereabouts are known, the adoption agency will inform the parent or guardian and, when it considers it is appropriate, the father of the child, of its decision.

ADOPTION PLACEMENT PLAN

Your adoption agency must create a written placement plan for you. The content of this is covered by the Adoption Agency Regulations 2005 and *must* include the following:

1. Whether the child has been placed under a Placement Order or with the consent of the parent or guardian.
2. The arrangements for preparing the child and the prospective adopter for the placement.
3. Date on which it is proposed to place the child for adoption with the prospective adopter.
4. The arrangements for review of the placement.
5. Whether parental responsibility of the prospective adopter for the child is to be restricted, and if so, the extent to which it is to be restricted.
6. Where the local authority has decided to provide adoption support services for the adoptive family, how these will be provided and by whom.
7. The arrangements the adoption agency has made for allowing any person contact with the child, the form

of contact, the arrangements for supporting contact and the name and contact details of the person responsible for facilitating the contact arrangements (if applicable).

8. The dates on which the child's life story book and later life letter are to be passed by the adoption agency to the prospective adopter.
9. Details of any other arrangements that need to be made.
10. Contact details of the child's social worker, the prospective adopter's social worker and out-of-hours contacts.

(Adoption Agency Regulations 2005 © Crown Copyright)

Your adoption agency is also required to provide, on request, an assessment of needs for your family and all of the members in it. It should include details of how you can obtain:

➤ advice, information and counselling
➤ financial support
➤ support through contact with groups for adoptive parents and children
➤ assistance with contact arrangements between your child and their birth relatives or other people important in your child's life prior to them being placed with you
➤ details of any therapeutic services available for your child
➤ details of services necessary to support you in your relationship with your child, including training and respite services

In the unlikely event that the placement breaks down, your agency is required to support you through the process of disruption and to examine the reasons why it happened in a sympathetic and healing way.

It is extremely helpful if you are able to put yourself in your child's shoes and try to chart their journey from birth to your family. All the information you receive from the adoption agency will help you do that. The next chapter looks at how you will set about finding your child – your ultimate goal that will make all the hard work worthwhile.

CHAPTER 7

The Selection Process

How do you choose one child over another? When you read about the children looking for homes, see their pictures and hear their distressing stories you will probably just want to scoop them all up and take them home. Sadly, there is a limit to what you can do. You have to listen to the head as well as the heart. You are doing more than your 'bit' by giving a loving home to someone who desperately needs it. By now you will have had a lot of time to decide what you are looking for in a child; stick to those criteria as best you can and try not to get too distracted. You know what, or who, you want so you have to harden yourself to making a choice based on your preferences.

At this stage it is best to get as much of this process under your control as possible in order to counter the months of powerlessness you will have experienced during the assessment. You should have a clear idea of the emotional, intellectual, financial, physical and practical resources you possess. Knowing what you have to offer will help you to choose.

Everyone involved in the matching process realises the importance of speed in placing a child with you. This must not compromise the agency's primary responsibility to ensure the best possible match. Adoption agencies will not cut corners; they do not want to risk an inappropriate or less than ideal match as this will increase the possibility that a placement will break down, which is in no one's interests. Therefore you may find that just as you are raring to go the process seems to grind to a halt. Don't worry; you must be prepared to wait. The system is endeavouring to ensure the best outcome. It has taken both you and your child a considerable length of time to get to this point, and while delay may seem unnecessary or overcautious, remember that adoption is for life. A few weeks' wait isn't unreasonable if you put it into this context. The aim is to have placed children with adoptive parents within 12 months of them becoming available for adoption. The time will relate to the type and age of the children involved. Your adoption agency should be able to give you a clear idea of the timescale they envisage.

The matching process can be upsetting. The profiles of children are often set out in brochures, a bit like a bizarre catalogue where the items on view are human beings. You will find yourself looking at hundreds of photographs and reading distressing details about children who have had terrible experiences. The case histories are likely to fire you with lots of emotions; everything from rage to pity. It may be that this is the first time you will have come across evidence of how badly people can treat vulnerable children. It can be a huge shock and may provoke anger towards parents who commit these abuses. These are normal, understandable reactions, especially as you are so centred on having a child. It is hard to comprehend how someone who has been given the gift of a baby can go on to treat them so badly. Use your sense of outrage to drive you on towards your goal of turning at least one of those lives around.

There are a number of publications that specialise in this field, such as *Be My Parent* and *Children Who Wait*. They feature profiles and pictures of children and groups of siblings of all ages and backgrounds who need adoptive or permanent foster families. *Be My Parent* started out as a monthly newspaper but is now also available online. It won the 2008 SustainIT eWell-Being Awards and was described as a 'tremendously effective and easy to navigate website which tugs on your heartstrings. A powerful medium for the delivery of the adoption message'. Each issue of *Children Who Wait*, run by Adoption-UK and open to Adoption-UK members, contains profiles of over 100 children waiting for parents. Another source is the local press. They often carry adverts about children or local events promoting adoption.

During this emotional process, hang on to the knowledge that you are not a helpless bystander; you are actually doing something that will make a huge difference. We have all sat on our sofa and shuddered at television news footage of starving children, reaching for the credit card to throw money at the problem. This is different. You are not passing on your guilt by giving to a charity for them to sort things out. This time you are rolling your sleeves up and doing the job yourself. As they say, the most effective charity begins at home.

Most people will be placed with a child from their local authority adoption agency. There is a 'general practice rule' that you will work with them to this end for at least three months. They will be aware of your abilities and know what post-adoption services you may require. It is more difficult to organise these services if you're adopting a child from a local authority in another part of the country or from abroad. This may also add to the time it takes to get a match. You may have chosen a voluntary agency for their faith-based or particular ethnic group expertise. If so, they will be well placed to help you find the sort of child or children you believe you will be able to care for.

The assessment programme will give you a general picture of the children you may adopt. It will specify, for example, whether it is one child or sibling groups, boys or girls, a specific age range or a child with particular disabilities. The current list of children up for adoption may also be restricted because of availability. It may be that the agency or local authority do not have someone who fits the profile you have put together. Your choice will be limited by these factors, which is why it is good to be flexible if necessary. Alternatively, you can wait until a child who fits the bill comes on to the adoption list.

Your social worker may have had a match in mind for you from day one. Indeed, you may have struck them as a perfect parent for a particular child. It's great if their instinct works out to be correct and the whole thing falls neatly into place. It does happen. There are quite a number of people other than you involved in the process of choice, such as the child, the child's social worker, your social worker, the adoption panel and finally the courts. But the most important players in this remain you and the child or children. At the end of the day, you are the ones who will have to live together. The choice is yours.

If you have not been matched within three months then

your local authority should pass your details to the adoption register. This is a database managed by social workers which has details of prospective adopters and children across England and Wales. It is their remit to try to match adopters and children who have been unsuccessful locally. Your local authority does not have to pass on your details so it is up to you to keep a close eye on developments. If you don't hear from the agency then chase them up. Don't worry about being a nag; this is too important a matter for you to sit back and wait for things to happen.

THOSE AROUND YOU

Do not forget those who have travelled this tricky road with you, such as your close family and friends. They will probably have shared your ups and downs, joys and sorrows. They will have invested love and time into the process and will want to share in the next crucial stage when you choose a child. Keep them up to date. Let them know your feelings as you face the uncomfortable task of selecting one person over another. It will be useful for them to see how hard it is, and it will illustrate the enormous benefits of what you are doing for the child. Let them feel they are also doing their 'bit' by keeping them in the loop.

You may be the cautious type who doesn't want to tempt fate by discussing your hopes of being matched with a particular child. If so, you don't have to be specific; you can speak generally about the choices in front of you. Those who love you will understand, so relax and enjoy being on the threshold of realising your dream of having a family.

BE REALISTIC AND STAY MOTIVATED

The key to managing this part of the adoption journey is to remain realistic and motivated. Now you can begin to allow yourself to get excited. Leaving the forms and formalities behind, you will start to prepare your house and your world for the reality of your child's arrival. At last, a chance to start 'nesting'. You will think about choosing and decorating the bedroom your child will occupy, and buying clothes and toys. You will probably wander around shops seeing things through new eyes – those of a parent. You will be reassessing the environment you live in with a view to what it can provide for your child, looking at local amenities such as playgroups, nurseries, mother and toddler sessions and, of course, schools. Parks and playgrounds take on a different relevance, as do local swimming pools, cinemas, indoor play centres, libraries and so on. Hunting around finding what is out there for your child can be an exhilarating experience. Enjoy it, and share it with your partner, family and friends.

MAKING A DECISION

The assessment and adoption preparation classes will have given you the intellectual information upon which to base informed decisions. However, the final decision – choosing your child – is likely to be emotional for most people. You are, after all, dealing with another human being. Unlike older children, babies come with an immediate need for care; indeed, their very survival relies on you, which is likely to trigger your innate human instinct to care for and protect them. Older children may seem less needy and come with a clearer and more obvious story. The process of learning about their plight, their journey to adoption and their needs is likely to augment your desire to want to help protect and nurture them; to offer them a better life, despite knowing, at some level, that you cannot predict how it will all work out.

Remember, those experienced in this area believe you will make good parents. They must be right, for at least 80 per cent of placements are successful. It is important to remember that your longing for a child will colour your view of your situation and your child, in part at least. It is only human to minimise in your mind the chances of problems occurring, and to overestimate your appraisal of your abilities to manage whatever comes your way. Do not let pride get in the way of your seeking help. Every professional in this field realises that everyone needs some help at some time, particularly as bringing up an adopted child is not like bringing up your biological child, whichever way you look at it.

Communication is vital. Once the adoption panel has approved a match the exchange of information begins in earnest. You will be itching to meet your child, and your excitement will be mixed with anxiety and apprehension. At this stage it is important to activate your support network of family and friends as you will need them as the matching and placement gets under way. It will be helpful if you know how best to play to their strengths, to get them to help you through the difficult times and be there to share the joyful times. They are part of your world and they will also be part of your new child's world in due course.

You may be lucky and everything will go smoothly and quickly. There is a great effort and desire to place children as quickly as possible, so you shouldn't need to wait more than 12 months after being approved to have a child placed with you. Things may not go as smoothly as you would wish, however, but hopefully you will have a clear idea about potential pitfalls before you start and how to deal with them. Whatever happens, and whatever the disappointments, remember that once you have been approved, you will be matched; of that have no doubt.

You could fall in love with a child from the outset or it may take time for this depth of feeling to develop fully, sometimes years. Like all relationships, this one can be entered into realistically or unrealistically, even after going through all the self-analysis of the assessment process. At first the matching is likely to be emotionally charged; it will only settle down with the passage of time and as you get to know each other better. The process of assessment is to ensure you make as informed a decision as possible; the reality of finding a child, or children, will be very exciting emotionally, especially as you are likely to have waited a long time for this opportunity.

WHEN THE MATCH IS NOT RIGHT

It is possible that the match is not right for numerous reasons. This could be apparent to you from early on. Of course, you will feel terrible if, for whatever reason, you cannot warm to your child but this is not the time to start pretending in order to keep everyone happy. Honesty has to be your rule. Unlike biological parenting, this is not a *fait accompli.* If the information you receive before you meet your child, or the impression or feelings you experience when you meet them, leave you in *any* doubt that the matching may not be right for you, you must, *at any stage of the process*, discuss this at the earliest possible opportunity with your social worker. Delay can only add to both your and your child's difficulties. Swift action should be taken as your child's welfare is paramount. The last thing anyone wants is to add to their emotionally difficult experiences.

The matching process in itself can be exciting. It is likely that your fantasies will be more grounded in reality having had access to a wealth of information about your child. You will feel you are almost there; almost a parent after all those months of assessment and preparation. Now your goal really is in sight and you are preparing to meet your child for the first time. The following chapter looks at what happens next.

CHAPTER 8

Meeting Your Child

This chapter will take you through the steps involved in meeting and getting to know your child. You will probably have all sorts of questions at this stage, and you should be able to find lots of helpful advice here. For example, there will be tips on how to prepare for meetings, where to have them and how to deal with your emotions. We will also look at good ways of communicating and providing information for your child.

THE FIRST MEETING

With an end in sight, or rather a new beginning, the moment has arrived when you will find yourself face to face with your child for the first time. You will have been made aware by your social worker that a match has been found, usually by phone. This means that quite a lot of work has gone on behind the scenes between your child's social worker and your own. If, however, you have 'spotted' a child you would like to adopt then you may be the driving force bringing together the social workers.

This is it! The culmination of the assessment process and the start of what you've wanted from the outset. This is perhaps the most exciting, nerve-wracking single occasion of the whole adoption process. So much is riding on it going well. First impressions are important, but not cast in stone. It may be love at first sight; then again it is just as likely to take a bit of time to develop strong feelings for each other.

Don't forget any of your own children, adopted or biological. They will be only too aware of what's happening. You will have involved them from the outset in your decisions and have made them an integral part of the whole plan. They will be excited but perhaps more apprehensive than you as they will be losing something: time. You will have less time for them as your next child will require special understanding and support in making their transition. You will therefore need to ensure you increase the one-to-one time with your own children to help them over this period and encourage them to talk openly with you about any concerns they may have. It will be an emotional juggling act and things may not go according to plan, but determination, openness, honesty and dialogue should win the day.

Remember that you are all in the same boat. Your child, depending on their age, will be just as nervous as you are about how things pan out. The professionals who have invested time and no doubt buckets of effort leading up to this will also be anxious that it works out well. The fact that this is really happening is likely to sink in at this stage. You are on the brink of taking a first step in a lifelong relationship. When you have that other person in front of you – the living, breathing embodiment of the child you have been thinking about for so long – the reality will be driven home to you. As life changes go, this is a biggy; possibly the biggest you will ever have the opportunity of choosing for yourself. By now you will have thrown so much into the adoption that it has become part of the jigsaw of your life; the only piece that has been missing is the child.

The meetings are not a haphazard series of encounters; they are carefully planned. One of the aims is for you to have the opportunity to observe, understand and learn the routines and behaviours that define your child. They also enable you to gently, yet firmly, insinuate yourself into a child's current world. This will help them make the move from where they are now into a new life in the least disturbing and most empowering fashion. This process is delicate, so do not rush it.

The first few meetings will have the awkwardness of a first date. You will worry about what to say to your child, even after rehearsing it over and over. It will be up to the social worker and foster parents to manage anxiety and tension. They will recognise how important the meeting is and aim to make it as light and enjoyable as possible for everyone concerned.

Much of the information you will have been given during your assessment will have concentrated on case studies of families with difficulties. These will have informed some of your discussions about what you might encounter with your adopted child. Remember that these case stories are generally focused on the most difficult and challenging issues you may face. Problems can come to dominate our thinking and colour our emotions. It is worth remembering that no one is *just* a sum of their problems. We all have strengths, even if we don't recognise them. It is essential to learn to identify and reward the good and positive aspects in your child in order to empower them and boost their self-esteem. Continued focus on difficulties and problems may only undermine us and our children and our abilities to overcome and succeed.

At the introductory meetings you will start to discover a lot about your child, such as:

> how they manage difficult situations
> what they really crave (and how they set about getting it)
> their habits
> their favourite foods
> how they interact with others

Observe, encourage and nurture their strengths, as it is through these that your child will find solutions to future difficulties. During the process of introductions include your child in all of the decisions that are being made about them. This gives them a clear message that they are integral to perhaps one of the biggest changes in their life to date.

Choosing your child is a rather surreal, magical experience and therefore difficult to quantify or describe. It is not generally one-sided; your child will be choosing you as much as you are choosing them. Have no doubt that your child will be assessing you from the outset. All you can do is be honest, open, flexible and consistent.

PREPARATION

This is something you will desperately want to get right. As with so many steps you have taken to date, preparation is vital. First meetings require a lot of careful and sensitive planning. The social workers involved on both sides will be geared up for this occasion; their experience of previous first meetings will be extensive and invaluable. They should put together a detailed introduction plan which you will be shown and to which you will have the opportunity to agree.

You might, however, feel confident enough to deal with this bit in your own way. After all, you will be taking the reins soon enough. It may be you don't want any more help or advice; you might have had enough of involving others in such a personal matter. While this is perfectly under-standable, it is best not to stumble at this last hurdle given the time and energy it has taken to get to this point. I would still counsel you to get as much information and advice as you can. You don't have to slavishly follow what you are told but it helps to have the information first so you can judge whether it is of any use or not. Bear in mind that you are heading into the unknown, whereas the professionals will have been at this point before. They will want to help; they are on your side so it is best to trust their judgement if you can.

While you are getting ready for the meeting, your child will also be carefully prepared. If they are old enough they will have been told about you. They may have seen photographs, a video or DVD. Their social worker and foster carer will have proceeded with sensitivity, trying to take away some of the enormous pressure the child will feel.

INTRODUCTIONS

Those who know and care for your child will dictate the tempo, duration and location of the first meeting. Initial introductions must not be too overwhelming, despite the likely level of anxiety and emotion felt by all parties. The social workers involved will have arranged for the meeting to take place in a neutral environment. They will keep an eye on the time, allowing you to concentrate on the child. Although you will be terribly nervous and want to impress, your focus should be on the child. Try to appear calm and be as true to your real self as possible in this tricky situation. This series of meetings will be to allow you and the child to test the ground, to see what it might be like when you live together.

Children are smart. If you want to bring presents, do so, but don't attempt to swamp them with gifts. The child may see this as an attempt to 'buy' their affections. It is best, perhaps, to treat them to something when out, such as an ice cream or a little memento of a visit. Reserve any special presents for times such as their first visit to what will be their new home. It is important to mark special occasions with tokens of love or commitment.

INTRODUCING YOUR CHILD TO YOUR HOME

After the initial contact the location of future meetings is likely to be your home. This enables you to demonstrate your daily routines, and it allows your child to see your home and begin to be familiar with it, particularly their own room. If they want to leave items for their next visit it is important to let them do so. Items should be left in their new personal space and may include a toothbrush, night clothes, toys you have got for them or their own special possessions. Be guided by your child in this matter. Make it easy for them to bring and leave what they want; this is all part of the progression. You should introduce your child to other family members, neighbours and friends. Pets will also be of interest and can be a wonderful ice-breaker.

The number of meetings before your child comes home permanently is usually in the region of six to eight weeks, but will be decided by your social worker, your child's social worker and you, and will be reviewed as events unfold. Although this will relate to the child's age and previous experiences, the process should not be unduly drawn out as this can add to uncertainty, particularly in your child's mind. The best starting position is little and often, as infrequent and overlong visits can become emotionally charged and a recipe for potential problems.

EMOTIONS

YOUR EMOTIONS

You may know or feel at once that this is the child, the only child, for you. This may be true but it may also be a result of coming face to face with a child who professionals believe could be yours after so many years of waiting and wanting. It will be difficult for you to suppress your excitement and emotions but you must try to do so in order not to overwhelm or scare your child. Oddly, such an important meeting may turn out to be an anticlimax, low key but quietly positive. On the other hand it may not work out. Remember, as much as you want things to go well, another human being is involved – a child – over whom you have no control. Generally, the best advice is to take things slowly and be patient. There is a lifetime ahead of you.

Prepare to be completely exhausted after the first meeting; it will certainly take it out of you emotionally. If you come away feeling wiped out, just try and imagine what the child must be going through. Your meetings will be draining, so anticipate this and make some special arrangements. Keep your diary clear for the rest of the day or do not go back to work. Just being aware of how you might feel will help. It will be important to try to think clearly at a time of heightened emotions. Hopefully, your partner will have taken time off work to be with you; that way you can run through how it went and clarify what you both feel at this point. Be honest. This is not a beauty parade; this is for keeps. So any problems, doubts or worries about the matching are best dealt with immediately, before hopes are raised only to be dashed. As the whole process can be emotionally draining, it is important to ensure that time is set aside for rest and contemplation. Generally, no matter how impatient you may feel, the best advice is to take things slowly; be patient. There is a lifetime ahead of you.

YOUR CHILD'S EMOTIONS

Your child is likely to have a longing for emotional warmth and comfort. They will also have had fantasies about what it will mean to have a new family. Depending on how old they are, they will have a picture in their mind of how it should be, possibly gleaned from books, television or films. They may be unrealistic in their beliefs and expectations; they are, after all, only children. Then again, you may have some fanciful beliefs and expectations of your own. It is important that you as the parent try to remain realistic while not crushing any dreams too harshly.

Your child is likely to feel torn in a few directions. On the one hand, they may be desperately keen to belong. On the other, they may have difficulties trusting and be fearful that things will not last. Small, emotionally neutral, safe steps and steady progress are vital for success. You may have to resist the temptation, overwhelming at times, to pick the child up and smother them with affection!

If you can, speak to all the adults involved in your child's life to date, particularly those who cared for them. This will help you to build up a realistic picture of their character and temperament, their likes and dislikes, strengths and weaknesses. Search for shared interests. Give your child time and space. Let them determine the pace of the initial meetings. Aim to make the move from foster care to your home as seamless as possible, taking the child with you at every step.

Your child will see the encounters from their own perspective. Their journey to this point has been hugely different to yours. Depending on their age they may have preconceptions as to how things will go; their expectations will be high, their need great. If you are dealing with an older child, be prepared for them to have mixed feelings as they are bringing more life experiences to the table. From the word go they will be testing boundaries, but then again, so are you.

The advice you have taken and the assessment you have been through should give you understanding, ideas, help and support as to how to manage these early meetings. Sensitivity to the child's needs is important, as is learning to read non-verbal cues. You are likely to be excited and apprehensive, as will your child – tell them, share it with them! It is important not to be overwhelming or over-emotional. Your child will be better than you at recognising non-verbal communications so you won't be able to hide much from them. Be honest and open, go slow and listen, listen, listen.

SHARING INFORMATION

The sharing of information with your child is extremely important, even before you meet. It is the responsibility of the social workers involved to provide you and the child with all the available information that will allow both of you to make an informed decision. The information may be available in a number of formats; particularly helpful would be a book of the child's life to date and possibly a video of them.

Provide the child with as much information as you can about who you are, who lives in your house, where it is, what it's like, what their bedroom will be like, any pets, extended family and so on. A video of your house and yourself and your extended family would be very helpful. You will want to reassure the child and give them some-thing to look forward to. Although you may be anxious, it is important to remember that, unlike biological parents, you have been found fit to be potential parents by specialists in this area. This should reassure and encourage you to be open and honest. All parents worry about their parenting skills at some stage but this is not the time to start. Enthusiasm, warmth and openness are infectious, so if you convey these feelings in any information you can give your child, this will help them see your joy at providing a forever family. This sharing of information is the beginning of a lifetime together. Take it slowly at the pace of the child or children and be realistic.

PART FOUR:

YOUR NEW FAMILY

CHAPTER 9

When Your Child Comes to Live with You

Just as you would prepare your home for a new baby, you will want to do some 'nesting' for your new child, perhaps painting their bedroom and putting in new furniture. If you have other children, they will be able to give you helpful advice about what your new child might like. You might want to spring-clean the house – do what feels right for you – but beware of making a rod for your own back. Your child may find your home daunting if it is too pristine. Let your child see the house as it is, which will hopefully appear lived in, warm and welcoming. Be excited – it is exciting – but also as relaxed as possible. Let your child feel special, that you have made an effort on their behalf, then help them settle into the natural rhythm of the home by getting on with things as you always do while making space for them to join in.

On a practical level, your child should have stayed at least a night or two in your home before they come to stay for good. This will allow them to get their bedroom the way they want it and get a good idea of the general layout of the house. They will also want to bring important objects from their past. Make this easy for them to do as having familiar things around them will help make them feel at home.

The child's homecoming is extraordinarily important and it is difficult not to make a big song and dance about it. However, it is better to ease your child in rather than having a party with a sea of new faces. This can be overwhelming for your child. Nevertheless, it is crucial to let the child know that their arrival is the subject of great joy and celebration, so just chugging on as normal as if nothing much has happened may be misconstrued as indifference. A balance must be struck. It might be worth taking advice from professionals and previous carers as to how best to do this. It does seem rather strange, and perhaps a bit sad, to have such a life-changing event and not be able to celebrate it other than in a low-key way. A compromise could be to have a series of small parties, gradually introducing your child to the key people in your life.

MANAGING CHANGE IN FAMILY DYNAMICS

A helpful way of thinking about families (or indeed relationships) is to see them as a system, a structured organisation where everyone has a particular role to play. If there is a problem with anyone in this organisation it will be reflected by a disturbance in the system's ability to function in a normal way. In a family, everyone interacts with each other in a shared positive, neutral or negative way. Families are complex; the interactions develop and become somewhat fixed in particular patterns over time. Therefore, your family will have developed a way of dealing with daily life. This will be changed when your child arrives. The more people you have in your family, the more your child will have to learn when they join you. It is a huge task so bear that in mind when you prepare everyone for the new arrival. The changes required after the addition of a child with special needs and disabilities are even greater. This process will take time and, in reality, never really stops. Change is a part of life; it is normal so accept it and work with it.

It is important for your child to feel they are joining a stable, secure and enduring structure that will be able to accommodate them and develop with their input and involvement. There will be enough change with this new addition so it is best to stick to your current ways of doing things and negotiate new ways rather than endeavouring to change everything.

YOUR RELATIONSHIP WITH YOUR CHILD

How you get on with your child or children will be the product of the bonds that grow between you. As with any parent–child relationship, it is not a negotiation of equals; you can be responsible only for what you bring to it. It is worth remembering that it is generally futile to try and get other people to change without changing yourself. This is particularly so with children. They will respond to change in you if this is consistent, enduring and clear.

The focus on relationships is key to the success of adoption. The desire to give and receive warmth, love, consideration and care is the reason why you wanted to become a parent. Your child is likely to bring with them memories of events and relationships from the past. Some of these memories will be positive but perhaps buried; few children, even from disadvantaged backgrounds, have unremittingly appalling experiences. Unsurprisingly, those children adopted later will have more emotional baggage and difficulties. They are more likely to have contact with other members of their birth family, siblings and friends from care, as well as having developed various coping strategies to help them survive in difficult times. Some of these mechanisms will be more effective than others and you will find out about them fairly quickly. Coping strategies are learnt behaviours that can be unlearnt given commitment, determination, time and patience.

SETTLING IN

When your child finally comes to stay with you the temptation will be to lavish them with everything, both emotionally and materially. This is something you have to rein in. You need to pace yourself and establish clear ground rules from day one – for you and the child alike. It is best to be cautious as the child has a lot to take on board. They have to become aware of, and get used to, the new constants in their life. The emphasis must be on constancy and consistency; after all, the lack of it in the past is the reason why they are being adopted. The child's age will dictate how you manage this. Once again, you will have planned for this time with your loved ones and social worker.

BRINGING HOME A BABY

If you are adopting a baby their needs will be obvious and basic: feeding, cleaning, sleeping, cuddling and playing. Despite the lengthy preparation for the moment when you become a parent for the first time, when it actually happens the reality will hit home with a force unlike anything you have experienced in the past. You have to some extent 'earned' this infant; they are here because of your determination to start a family. Like any realisation of a dream, however, the moment it comes true is never quite as you planned. Early on there will be whistles and bells, joy and celebrations, enormous feelings of love and compassion – exactly the same as for a birth parent. There comes a time, however, when the bouquets have wilted and the champagne bottles sit outside in the recycling bin, and the reality of actually being a parent sets in. This bit can be quite scary, daunting and even lonely. You will have thought through all the pitfalls as well as the delights of parenting but there is a huge difference between seeing it on paper or working it through in your head to actually doing it in practice.

Your emotions will be many and varied. You may experience great highs and lows all in the space of a few hours. With euphoria may come a tinge of the blues. Having been through an intense period of working with the agency to get this far you will now feel as though you are on your own without the paraphernalia, scrutiny and the safety of the assessment process. You may be delighted that at last it is just you and your child; then again, you may have mixed feelings. This is normal and to be expected. After all, just think about what you have gone through to become a parent. You have come a long way, and to some extent the journey is only just beginning. The idea of never being able to go back can be difficult. Your time to choose is in the past; now you can only go ahead. Don't forget, however, that it is important to share your thoughts and seek advice. There are plenty of people around you, either professionals or family and friends, who will be more than happy to give you support and good guidance. You are not alone; actually, you have more help to hand than many birth parents, so use it.

BRINGING HOME AN OLDER CHILD

Bringing home an older child is quite a different matter. Yes, they do have basic needs but you have to factor much more into the equation as they also have a past, a time out of your control that will have moulded who they are now. If your child is very young, you may not know what exactly happened to them; after all, they will not be good witnesses. In all children, you will need to be as sensitive as you can in dealing with any issues that arise from the past. Never force a child to relive painful events unless they choose to do so. To some extent, a good way ahead is to regard this as a fresh start for your child. Yes, there are past complications which shouldn't be ignored, but by the same token we all have to get on with life and make the best of things. A healthy, positive approach with an emphasis on a bright future will work wonders.

By the time your child moves in, you will hopefully have a good grasp of what you are dealing with in terms of their past and the place they have come from. Older children may find the adjustment a bit more complicated and present you with different challenges. It will be important to seek and accept help if things are not working out as you would have hoped.

ESTABLISHING ROUTINES

Organising a routine for your child, particularly when it comes to schooling, will give them the message that you're committed to their future, not only in your life but in the local community too. This activity will also make you start to feel like a real parent. If you have a school-age child you need to plan the timing of the placement carefully. For example, your child might be placed towards the end of a school term so you could introduce them to a new school and their new classmates at a time when there is likely to be an end-of-term feeling. Both you and your child could start to meet the teachers and other pupils on a few mornings.

You may well have spoken to teachers at a local school about your proposed adoption, but you do not have to share this information if you don't want to. Schools and teachers are now much better at understanding, discussing and accepting diversity, particularly in inner city areas. School-children are often encouraged to discuss their family life and where they've come from, so you need to be happy that your child's teacher understands their background and adoption.

Routines and rituals are important and are dictated by many factors such as work, school, pets and family commitments. It is a good idea to create new rituals with your child. Mealtimes are an excellent opportunity to bond. Sitting down together in the evening and talking about the experiences of the day over food is a pleasure for all.

BROTHERS AND SISTERS

If you already have children, the experience of adopting a new child will be no less life changing or exciting but you will at least have some experience to call upon. You are unlikely to have got this far without your existing children's approval and support. Both you and your social worker will have discussed the possibility of an adopted child with them. In all UK adoptions, any other children in the family are involved in the assessment and decision-making process. They will be asked for their opinions on the parenting and nurturing experiences you have provided for them.

Few, if any, adoption agencies will recommend the placement of a child who is less than two years younger than your youngest child. If your current child or children are also adopted they may welcome the prospect of another adopted child as it can confirm their normality, or the normality of the process at least. Your current child can provide your new child with a ready-made source of information about your family and how it works, its strengths and weaknesses, its checks and balances and an introduction to the uncharted world of the extended family and friends. All is made easier for your new child when there are few family tensions or difficulties, and attachments and bonding are secure.

Sibling rivalry is normal and necessary in the development of children's understanding of sharing, helping and the separateness of others and their needs. Children adopted into a family where they have ready-made brothers and sisters are spared the constant scrutiny and glare of first-time parents' anxieties. However, your new child will have the difficult task of negotiating their place in your family and fitting in with their new brothers and sisters. It is asking an awful lot of your adoptive child and your current children to adjust to this change. The transition is unlikely to be completely smooth as everyone may have to learn a set of new skills. While things may seem right in theory, the reality may prove different and more challenging, particularly after any initial honeymoon phase.

All of your immediate family will be involved in the introductions and meetings prior to placement, as well as in the information given to your potential child. As much as you will be anxious to reassure your new child they will fit in, they will be only too aware and anxious about their role in the unfolding drama. Honesty, openness and flexibility are vital. The process, with its attendant emotional baggage, must be dealt with in a sensitive way that normalises the experience for all concerned and tolerates the occasional hiccup without upsetting the apple cart. Your own children will require extra support as they negotiate the changes in the balance of the family and the new relationships involved.

Depending on the level of neglect and/or abuse suffered by your new child, it will be important to help your current children understand a bit about their new brother or sister and why they may have some particular needs. You are likely to need professional help with this aspect of preparing your current children. It is essential to reassure them that they remain special, and that the relationship you have built up with them is strong and unchanging. This will be important should you or your current children be faced with any particularly challenging emotions or behaviours from your adopted child.

Understanding the normality of sibling rivalry is important if you are to remain relaxed about it. If you spot it, talk about it. Be sensitive to the needs of your own children who may find adjustment difficult and become frustrated. This may spill over into unhelpful behaviours. Explore the context of any problems and give all those involved the chance to talk, individually and together. Secrets fester and corrode. Openness, clarity, sympathy, understanding and fairness will win the day. However, do not be afraid to lay down the law when, or if, behaviours are unacceptable.

Once your child has settled into your home and your routine, you can get on with enjoying life as a new family. You will gradually get to know your child better and the bond between you will strengthen. In the next chapter we look at issues of bonding as well as some of the parenting challenges specific to adoption that may crop up.

CHAPTER 10

Parenting

The granting of the Adoption Order is an extremely important day. It is like a birthday. You are now legally a parent. Families celebrate this in different ways but it is an important milestone for everyone involved in what is likely to have been a long and arduous journey. Now is the time to begin the task of day-to-day parenting. In this chapter we will look at many aspects of parenting, some general and others specific to adopted children.

BEING A 'GOOD-ENOUGH' PARENT

This is a good time to bring the psychoanalyst D.W. Winnicott back into the picture. As I mentioned in Chapter 5, he came up with the concept of 'good-enough' parenting. It is a strong, realistic and attainable goal. Conversely, there are many ways of being a bad parent. Most parents think they are bad or not good enough from time to time. Bear in mind, though, that perfect parents do not exist. There are certainly parents who are better than others, and perhaps most of us could always do better. If you think this then you're probably doing okay; if you think you're perfect you're probably not.

It is important to be realistic about your parenting skills and abilities. It's not just you in this equation; your children will have a say and so you will not be able to control things as perhaps you would like to. Although it doesn't sound very aspirational, aim to be a 'good-enough' parent as opposed to the fictional perfect mother or father.

Parenting is a complicated job. Before a child is placed with you as adoptive parents, you are likely to have thought the whole process through from beginning to end in great detail. Indeed, you are probably better prepared than most biological parents, particularly as you have a strong team alongside to support and guide you. After all the preparation, you should have some understanding about how your interaction with your child is reciprocal and how you will affect each other, particularly when you hit a rocky patch. At such times emotions can run high; hurtful things may be said or thought and you may come to question your parenting skills. There will probably be times when, just like biological parents, you would like to give the child back but – as with biological children – once adopted, they're yours. These troubles may feel desperate but they are a normal part of parenting; this kind of mini-crisis is what brings you together. Surviving the bad makes the good so much better. One of the characteristics of good parenting, and indeed most solid relationships, is when everyone involved can successfully negotiate difficult times and come out stronger.

As you get to know your child, you will come to under-stand their side of the relationship better. You will become aware of their biologically given temperament, and how there are some aspects of their personality that are unlikely to change and are best accepted. While this is the same for biological parents, as adoptive parents you may be more inclined to blame any difficulties you might be experiencing on your failings rather than inherent qualities in your child. The opposite scenario may be true, where you blame the child's genetic make-up rather than take on board that the situation has a lot to do with your handling of it. Children and parents have to accept some givens and adjust expectations of each other accordingly.

Some adoptive children come with a number of complex issues from their past. Some will have been traumatised or physically and sexually abused. It is possible that these experiences will reveal themselves in disturbed relation-ships, not only with you but also with your other children. When these issues come to light, hopefully before you've adopted your child, they're likely to require professional intervention which should pay attention to your needs as a family group. These sort of disturbed relationships are not really sibling rivalry; they are something else and must be treated in a different way.

Those in your extended family as well as your friendship circle will be aware of the effects your child has upon you and your family. As with most friends and families, everyone will have a view about how it's going and how you are coping. Some families get on better than others, and if you are having difficulties you will probably be able to understand people's motives when they're discussing your situation. It's important to remember why people say what they say and not to fall into the trap of misinter-preting or misusing their words to add to any self-critical trait you may possess about your parenting skills. If you can spot an argument coming, it's best to be able to head it off as quickly as possible.

Remember, no one gets parenting 'completely' right; everyone makes mistakes. The emotional roller coaster that is child-rearing is similar for biological and adoptive parents. Occasionally the process is enjoyable enough to be knowingly repeated!

CHILD DEVELOPMENT

Improved knowledge and understanding of childhood development has led to changes in thinking about adopting and adoptive parents. The assessment process will look at your formative psychological and social experiences, for example, and see how these might help or hinder you in your desire to parent an adopted child. It may be that your child's emotional state and challenging behaviours resonate with issues from your past and disturb your relationships.

A child's progress is monitored using age-appropriate developmental markers. In other words, you will be able to judge how well your child is doing through comparisons. You will need to know the sort of milestones we are talking about; these can be gleaned from professionals such as health visitors, GPs and paediatricians but also from websites and books. For example, one of the areas that can be monitored is your child's social relationships – within the home, at school and with their peer group. The sort of physical and intellectual activities your child enjoys will also tell you how they are doing.

It may be that when your child came to you they were

behind the developmental curve as a result of physical, social or emotional neglect or abuse. Once they settle down, you will have the pleasure of seeing them start to fulfil their potential, and watch as they catch up with their peers. This will also be a great boon to your child as it will add to their understanding of the clear benefits of their adoption.

Aspects of child development will be covered during the assessment/education process but it is important to seek out as much information as you can. Aim to put yourself in a good position to understand about your child and what is normal for their age in social, physical, emotional and psychological terms. You will become aware of what your child can and cannot do when they are first placed with you. As time passes you may become less observant if they reach their milestones without problems and develop normally.

If your child has developmental problems, don't wait too long before identifying them and getting help. If you are at all worried at any stage, seek advice from your GP, health visitor, social worker or anyone else involved in your child's care. There may have been pointers to potential future difficulties that you should have discussed with your social worker and the child's social worker before you adopted, making appropriate arrangements for follow-up and help. It might be worth reviewing your own documents to see if something was missed that may be of relevance now. For instance, dyslexia in the biological family would be highly relevant to any problems your child may be having in school.

Sometimes developmental delays and difficulties reveal themselves only as time passes. You will frequently be made aware of how your child is doing in comparison with their peer group. Problems may, however, only become obvious for the first time when children start nursery or junior school.

DEVELOPMENTAL MILESTONES

At whatever age you adopt a child you will have missed their attainment of certain important developmental milestones. You are also likely to have missed learning about your child's temperament. Some babies are naturally placid, some energetic, others fractious, fretful and irritable, traits which may persist and be misattributed to environmental experiences rather than something inherent. You may make the mistake of thinking that these traits can easily be changed. Sadly, some of them are hardwired. It is important to understand this as there is little point in trying to change something so fixed. The best approach is to acknowledge and accept these traits and work around them.

Children grow and develop in physical, emotional, social, language and cognitive areas. These developments do not necessarily always occur at the same age, and will be disturbed if the child is subject to neglect, deprivations and abuse. If we take the average age of four as the likely age of the child you will adopt then your child should be able to:

➤ dress or undress themselves
➤ throw a ball over-arm
➤ jump up and down
➤ pedal a bicycle with/without stabilisers
➤ hold a crayon between thumbs and fingers
➤ scribble

- stack four blocks
- construct sentences of three words
- show interest in interactive games
- respond to people outside the family
- engage in fantasy play
- use the toilet appropriately
- use 'me' or 'you' appropriately in sentences

In addition, four-year-old children:

- are usually not clingy and do not cry if separated from carers or parents
- do not ignore other children
- do not resist dressing or sleeping
- do not get inappropriately angry or distressed

Before your child is considered for adoption, any delay in their attainment of the age-appropriate developmental milestones should, where possible, be identified. This should lead to a full assessment, and you must be made aware of this before the child is placed with you.

Try to find out if any delays in attaining milestones are a result of the circumstances of the child's life experiences to date or whether they are specific learning difficulties in their own right. This distinction is crucial but may not become clear until some time after your child has been placed or adopted; it is a risk you will knowingly accept. It is only natural to think the worst if you have little knowledge, but even I as a doctor can easily worry unduly when my children are having problems. I have to remind myself (as well as junior doctors and patients) that 'common things occur commonly'. Think simple things first. So, for example, hearing or visual impairment may account for developmental delays or behavioural and emotional exasperation. Another relatively common condition, dyslexia, may not reveal itself until later.

Even though you will not have known your child from birth, you are likely to see enormous improvements in their attainments and development after they are placed with you and settle into your family. Their improvements frequently surprise health and social work professionals. This, after all, is why you adopt; to give a child, or children, the nurturing and environment necessary to develop physically, socially, emotionally and intellectually and achieve their potential. If your child is disabled, and their developmental difficulties and delays are well known, remember they too will improve in a loving family. However, the timescale and progress will be different, so goals must be realistic and attainable.

Although genes are important, their expression is heavily influenced by a complex interaction with the environment. The old debate of nature versus nurture is spurious in most cases, except in well-known and rare genetic deficiencies. It is the provision of a loving, caring family to adulthood and beyond that is vital to your child, no matter what their genetic burden.

PARENTING VULNERABLE CHILDREN

It is easy to forget how important behaviour is. No matter what age we are we frequently express ourselves, and judge others, through behaviour. As adults we have the use of language but not everyone is able to express themselves emotionally in a coherent, positive way, particularly without training or good role models. Children are most likely to reveal themselves through their behaviour. The way they do this will depend on their age and character as well as their physical, social and emotional development. Talking about worries and seeking help is more problematic for those who have difficulty trusting other people. It will be particularly difficult for children who have been belittled, derided or exploited in the past when trying to confide in others. Some children may find it difficult to express themselves verbally because of problems such as learning difficulties.

Parenting vulnerable children is not easy. The road can be a rocky one but it is worth the journey. You will have your work cut out, primarily building a relationship with the child based on trust. You need to make them feel valued, secure and able to risk exposing their vulner-abilities. Only through doing this will your child achieve their full potential. It helps to take a philosophical approach to life, especially when considering how your child was treated before coming under your wing. You will be able to come to terms with what happened to your child in the past if you can take on board the limitations of some humans, particularly those who are unable to care for their children and who may not understand the damage they may have inflicted. Compassion and acceptance of the human state implies a level of maturity that bodes well for you and your child.

How you cope will have an impact on your child. It is therefore important to be able to hang on to hope and instil this in your child. This requires a positive, yet realistic view of the future and what may be achieved. You may well be surprised as your child grows through your nurturing, but don't expect a transformation overnight. Be realistic and remember that this undertaking is for life; there is no quick fix to what has gone on in your child's past. There will be good and bad times. It can take many years for your new addition to adapt, to unlearn the behaviours they have had to cling on to in order to survive. Give the child, yourself and your family group the time they need to achieve some equilibrium. Have faith that this will happen. Don't give up. Churchill was fond of saying, 'When you are going through hell just keep going.' Life's experiences bear this out.

DEALING WITH CHALLENGING EMOTIONS AND BEHAVIOURS

The key to managing a challenging behaviour is to put it into context. Short-term behavioural upsets are completely normal. When challenging behaviours become difficult and persistent they are a sign that help is needed. It is useful to remember that such behaviours are learnt and can thus be unlearnt and replaced, in time, with more positive and healthy coping strategies.

Challenging behaviours differ from the normal testing of boundaries that all children do at some stage. One of the ways children learn is through 'modelling'. This consists of what you do, how you do it and how it relates to what you say. Therefore, from the moment your child joins you, be aware that your words must reflect your actions. So, for example, if you say 'no' but do not back this up through your actions, be prepared for potential trouble at some stage. Setting reasonable and clear boundaries, gently but firmly, from the outset is important as they provide structure and safety for children. They are vitally important to the healthy development of personality and character.

All children test boundaries on a regular basis, pushing against them to see if they are still firm. This is particularly true as they move into adolescence. Your child may have had little or no experience of consistent and fair boundaries and an overabundance of arbitrary, inconsistent and inappropriate ones. Be prepared to be sensitive to your child's needs while taking into account the needs of others who will also have to accommodate them. This can be where the 'labour' in labour of love comes from!

Challenging behaviours are difficult and demanding to manage, whether physical, psychological or social. It is essential to recognise the cost for all members of your family, especially your other children. During the evaluation and educational phases of your assessment you will have been made aware of emotional and behavioural disturbances in some adoptive children. You will also have considered, in theory at least, what behaviours you will or will not be able to manage. If they are going to happen, challenging behaviours may manifest themselves from the outset, or after a honeymoon period during which all parties will have been assessing each other. It will be important to seek advice early, to nip the behaviours in the bud where possible but also to ensure that you believe you are doing the right thing, using the right tools and help from those experienced in this area. You may wish to extend your understanding of the subject through either your local authority adoption agency or organisations such as BAAF (see Resources, page 248).

Your new child will want to know you'll be there for them through thick and thin, yet initially, at least, they are unlikely to believe you will be. You should be prepared to accept that they will put this to the test at some stage. It will hurt. It is important, however, to try and understand what is happening and to recognise what lies behind the behaviour. One way of doing this is to conceptualise the behaviour as a communication or symptom of some distress. For example, aggression may follow situations where your child feels frustrated, helpless or fearful. These emotions and thoughts may be quite brief and can be lost as the adult's attention is directed towards the behavioural manifestations of anger. Contemplation that some emotions or thoughts may occur before the anger will help you feel less personally attacked as well as offering your child and your family a way of under-standing, and managing, such outbursts. It may also help to remember that your child's experiences may, consciously or unconsciously, remind them of some unpleasantness in their past and you may possibly be in receipt of residual anger that they have been unable to direct towards individuals who have harmed them in their previous life.

Knowing what lies at the root of the behaviour can be empowering for everyone involved. Although this does not necessarily make the experience any less painful, it gives you a starting point from which to explore solutions. Remember once more, unlike biological parents, you have been assessed by professionals who believe that you are likely to have all the qualities that one can reasonably expect in 'good-enough' parents; you don't have to be perfect. Unless you are quite deluded about your parenting skills, it is only natural to feel quite useless from time to time when confronted by your badly behaved children, particularly when this occurs in public. Swallowing pride and realising that we're not perfect and do get things wrong from time to time can be very helpful. Recognising your limits, while painful, offers you the chance of personal growth. If handled with maturity and support, this is likely to improve your parenting skills and relationship with your children, and help them wrestle their demons from the past.

It is unhelpful to blame either yourself or the child for everything that has gone wrong. As with most relationships it is best if everyone can understand and take responsibility for their actions. As an adult you will be in a much better position than your adopted child to do this. Your actions will speak louder than words and form a good role model as you help them understand the consequences of their behaviour while remaining constant and caring in your relationship with them.

Before coming to you, your child may have been the scapegoat of poor parenting and disturbed relationships. They may have been left with the feeling that they were fundamentally wicked or bad, having been told this numerous times. It is likely to have been easier to believe this rather than run the risk of further abuse or neglect and alienation from what little parenting they were receiving at the time. Indeed, it is not uncommon for children to idealise poor or abusive parents.

So, do not take things personally. Easily said but difficult in practice when your child is being especially hateful and pressing all the emotional buttons you didn't even know existed but they have spotted. It may not be you the person that is being attacked; it is you the adult and what you represent. When things are tough and the child is struggling, you may come to represent (just) another adult from their past life who may have been inconsistent and abusive and have let them down. You may never be fully able to know or understand what happened to your child before you met them. Indeed, the child may not be able to articulate what they are thinking or feeling other than in an eruption of unfocused emotion and indiscriminate challenging behaviour. This is a challenge to your understanding, acceptance and tolerance – not your authority. You are being put to the test, not necessarily consciously; how you respond will help all of you move forwards.

GETTING HELP

If your child's challenging behaviours are persistent, you will need professional support. Your local authority social workers should be able to help you with this. It is fundamentally important to be able to step out of, or step back from, the emotional immediacy of the problem and identify the events that trigger such behaviours. Once you recognise these triggers you can start to address them.

There are now numerous excellent resources about parenting that can encourage, enlighten and help you. The BBC and Channel 4 websites provide simple, clear and concise advice as well as excellent links to further relevant parenting sites (see Resources, page 248). For 'difficult' children, programmes like 'Super Nanny' (Channel 4) are both entertaining and instructive. You will see that the 'expert' targets both parents *and* children, and transformations come from the consistent application of boundaries in nearly every case. Such programmes can provide you with the evidence that behaviours can change through consistency and perseverance; seldom is rocket science involved.

However, changing habits is not easy for anyone, even a toddler. It requires single-mindedness, total commitment and family solidarity in the face of challenges. Everyone in your family unit is involved. Although your child may feel you are 'ganging up' on them, this is not the case. You are looking to extinguish behaviours that are damaging to your child, your other children and your family unit, while at the same time offering your new child affectionate, safe and secure boundaries.

It's easy to get bogged down in what's wrong. It is equally important to actively seek out what's right, and reward it with time, intimacy, sharing and doing things together. Remember, children are excellent 'readers' of non-verbal communications and can pick up on your emotions – when you feel proud, tell them; when you feel love, show them. Reward the good and positive whenever it occurs. Come to understand your child's strengths by observing them, and then help them to develop them.

MANAGING MEALTIMES

Many parents have to deal with difficult behaviours when it comes to their children's eating habits. Giving and receiving is a powerful metaphor, and eating or not eating can be used as a way of communicating distress. Food is thus an extremely important and symbolic part of our daily routine. Given its core importance in 'feeding' and nurturing, it can become a focus for conflict which may be better addressed elsewhere.

Try to organise your life so that there are times when you all sit down together to eat. Have a clear idea of your child's likes and dislikes before they move in and make mealtimes enjoyable; preparing and eating meals together may be a new experience for your child. With care, determination and tolerance, it is possible to change eating habits. In order to change your child you are also likely to need to address, or at least understand, your own relationship with food and eating. This is an area where professional advice may be worth obtaining sooner rather than later.

BEING YOUR CHILD'S 'THERAPIST'

You will have been through a lot of assessment and scrutiny by the time the child has been placed with you, and this will continue at least until the Adoption Order is made. It may be that you are heartily fed up with the process and just want to be left alone to be a parent. While biological parents may need to take on the role of therapist from time to time, it is a role for which few of them will have had any preparation. They will pick it up as they go along and generally won't have had to contemplate the prospect of challenging behaviours, other than the occasional testing of boundaries. You, on the other hand, may have already contemplated the need to step out from the 'simple' role of parent and embrace some aspects of being a therapist. Any foray into this realm should be temporary. It is important to relinquish this role as rapidly as possible as a child needs a parent, not a therapist; and you need a child, not a client.

However wrong the term 'therapist' may feel, it is perhaps a useful way of thinking about some of the skills you need as an adoptive parent, or indeed any parent. Contemplate what therapists can do and what you can learn from them. They aim to listen in a dispassionate way to a description of difficulties; to look for patterns and appropriate, consistent and agreed solutions. They can offer a non-judgemental way of seeing a situation in a different light or from a different perspective; where problems can be explored; where explanations and under-standing are sought and where blame is not apportioned.

When contemplating challenging behaviours it is perhaps important to start observing and understanding your child at times when they are well, settled, content and happy. What is it about these times, or situations, that differ from challenging times? It is important to understand what motivates your child and what they most want in terms of rewards. I'm not discussing or recommending financial rewards. In fact, what your child desires most is time with you, especially having you all to themselves. They want time to share and time to be heard. If you know what the child enjoys most you can use this as a reward for good behaviours.

When things are difficult you may just have to ride the

storm until calm returns. If possible, step out of the situation and see if there is anything triggering misbehaviour that you can easily and quickly change. Once calm is restored, analyse what happened and how it happened; look for the triggers and see what you can learn from this. If sensitively and patiently handled, it should, with time, be possible to work with your child in untangling the history of their behaviours. See if you can utilise the knowledge you gain from such situations to inform your behaviour and help you not to reinforce the behaviours by your reactions. The best way to extinguish bad behaviours is to, as far as is humanly possible, ignore the bad and reward the good. The rewards should be those things you have noticed your child enjoys the most or those you and your child have agreed upon beforehand. This is known as operant conditioning. It is not easy; but it works.

Knowledge of your child's background will be very important in how you handle challenging behaviour. Talk to as many carers who have looked after your child as possible to glean as much information as you can about their strengths and coping strategies. Written information is likely to inform you of the type of abuse or neglect they may have suffered, but face-to-face talking with those who have experience of your child is invaluable. This may save you and your child much time and heartache. For example, sending a child to their room may have a massively different connotation for a child from an abusive background than for another child who has not had this dreadful experience. Similarly, close proximity at times of distress may be misconstrued by such children. Try to remain flexible and open to trying out different ideas. It's also important to think outside the box. Your child's bad behaviour may, for example, relate to a physical problem like an illness, pain or difficulty with hearing or sight. Again, always seek advice if you are unsure.

Ensure your child knows what is acceptable through your actions. Your actions must reflect your words if they are to provide a constant and clear message that informs your child where the boundaries are so they can feel safe, wanted and loved. Some children and some behaviours try the patience of the numerous parent-saints out there. You are not alone. Remember, you only need to be 'good enough'.

DEALING WITH CHALLENGING BEHAVIOURS IN PUBLIC

One of the problems with challenging behaviours is where they happen. A temper tantrum in a supermarket is very different from a temper tantrum at home. When you are outside the home you are subject to a vastly different series of social pressures which create embarrassment, frustration and irritation. A child with challenging behaviours is likely to know this at some level and will react to your social discomfort and anxiety in a way that is not likely to make you feel any better. In these circumstances you may feel particularly insecure or inadequate in your parenting skills. Be reassured: this happens to all families, be they biological, foster or adoptive.

PSYCHOTHERAPY

If your child has been neglected, abused or traumatised they may require help from child and adolescent mental health services. They may be offered psychotherapy in order to enhance their abilities to relate to you and achieve their full potential. This does not mean that you are a bad parent. Psychotherapy will help your child come to terms with difficulties from their past, not their present. It is used with children whose past traumas are revealing themselves through emotional and behavioural difficulties in the present. You may need help in your own right to understand and support your child as they go through therapy. Sometimes your family will be offered therapy.

The need for therapy may only become clear as your child begins to relate to you and feel safe enough to be able to discuss some of these issues from the past. Your family needs should be reassessed at the point at which it becomes clear that issues from the past are intruding into the present. On the other hand, you may already know about your child's needs in this area. Any issues related to your child's mental health needs must be made clear to you at their placement and contained in the Adoption Placement Plan. This is an important area as it may stir up issues related to your own childhood experiences. Only a minority of people have deeply troublesome childhood events and so your understanding may be limited. To understand these things more fully, ask your adoption agency for further information and details of training courses.

BONDING WITH YOUR CHILD

You will have learnt about bonding during your Home Study and any educational sessions you have attended, and you will have discussed it with your social worker. Nothing, however, can teach you about the 'chemistry', the mixture of physical and emotional sensations experienced when you meet and start to live with your child every day.

Some adoptive parents will feel an attachment to a child at once. Sometimes one adoptive parent feels a greater attachment to a child than the other. This can set up a disturbed dynamic in your relationship which must be addressed as soon as it is noted. In a similar way, a child may attach better to one parent than the other. Some children, particularly if they are disturbed, are able to switch allegiances and set parents against each other. This is called 'splitting'. It can be very destructive and must be tackled early and firmly. If you feel this is happening, seek professional advice as you may require specialist help.

When your child leaves their foster parents, it is actually a good sign if everyone is upset. It signifies that your child has the ability to form relationships and therefore bodes well for the placement. It may not be love at first sight. After placement, and indeed adoption, there can be a sort of anticlimax when you come face to face with the realities of looking after a child full-time. It is worth remembering that although you are 'new parents' you have come to parenting perhaps later in life than many biological parents, so you will have more experiences on which to fall back. Bear in mind, too, that your child is also likely to have come to their new family relatively late in their life. Just like you, they will have some experiences that will inform their beliefs, behaviours and hopes. Unfortunately, however, their experiences may have been less positive than yours.

Relationships are two-way traffic. Building them takes

place at many levels, and changes in response to events and the passage of time. It is asking a lot of your child to share their intimate feelings and secrets until they feel safe in trusting these with you. Once again, it will help if you can put yourself in their shoes and try to understand how – and perhaps even what – they are thinking. For example, they may feel that they would be betraying their previous carers or parents if they were to show you too much emotion too quickly, or they may feel embarrassed by some of the thoughts and feelings they have.

You may feel your child holds all the cards, to start with at least. It is not always possible to run things the way you would like them to be. Remember, help is at hand if you need it. Speak to your social worker or health visitor if you have worries about how you are bonding with your child. Don't wait until things have become very difficult as it's easier to fix things earlier than later. Try to stay in touch with your needs and your thoughts, and don't let pride get in the way of asking for help for yourself and your child.

You cannot be perfect. Children can be trying at times for any parent, particularly when challenging and testing boundaries through their behaviours. No one feels good all the time; everyone is allowed to snap sometimes. This is normal. Do not add to your difficulties by trying to be perfect all the time; it's impossible. Children need to know that you have your limits and that there is a time for them to step back. This is likely to be more difficult for children from disadvantaged backgrounds.

Sometimes children behave perfectly when out visiting friends or health professionals but appallingly at home. In these situations, you may feel that others do not believe you. Such thoughts can reinforce any negative beliefs you have about your parenting skills. Once again, seek help early. Your experiences are real and will be understood by people and professionals who know about children from disadvantaged, neglectful and abusive backgrounds. Their validation will be extremely important for you.

Remember, you are only human and can only ever be a 'good-enough' parent. Accept that you have taken on a very difficult and challenging job. You are doing one of the most wonderful things any human can do for another. Unlike biological parents, you have been through a rigorous assessment procedure and found to have all the attributes to make a 'good-enough' parent for some of the most disadvantaged of all small humans.

PART FIVE:
THE FUTURE

CHAPTER 11

Your Child's Past

As you look forward to sharing your future with your adopted child, you will need to be aware that at some stage your child is likely to want to know about their past. Whether we are adopted or not, our past is vitally important in helping us form a concept of our identity. If you are at ease with the subject, you will unquestionably help your child to have a workable relationship with their past. In this chapter we will look at issues such as how to explain to your child that they were adopted, and how to manage contact with their birth family.

ASKING AND TELLING

Your child is bound to bring up the question of their biological family sooner or later. They are likely to have discussed it with their social worker before meeting you at the very least, if they were old enough to do so. As adoptive parents you will have thought about how to deal with this issue when it arises. You may dread this or welcome it; either way you will have to deal with it. Try putting yourself in your child's position and understand what they are thinking and feeling. Remember not to misinterpret enthusiasm to find out about their biological parents as a rejection of you. Such questions should be sensitively encouraged.

Your child's interest may simply be a need to know. This may or may not develop into something more, such as direct contact. Adopted children will have mixed feelings about their biological parents, which may range from detesting them to idolising them. They may fantasise about their biological parents, particularly when things are difficult. These days, everyone involved in looking after your child before they came to you will have talked with them about their past. Your child's awareness of issues relating to their birth family will change with time, as will their ability to deal with them. It will be up to you to help them manage this with sensitivity, understanding, tolerance, perseverance and love. You may even want to meet the biological parents. If so, seek advice to help you make an informed decision. Consult your nearest and dearest too, as they will be the ones to prop you up if this venture goes pear-shaped.

It is best to deal with questions as and when they crop up, manage them at that time and be guided by your child and what you know of them. There should be no specific time when your child can recollect being told they were adopted. You can prepare the ground by talking about it from the outset, normalising the whole issue of adoption. In order to do this you need to be comfortable with the whole subject because, whatever you say or however you say it, your child will pick up the nuances and any difficulties you may be having.

The first and most important thing to remember is to go

at your child's pace: slowly. Talk about the past in an interested, non-judgemental way using their life-story book (see page 221). Listen to, and talk about, their tales, trials and tribulations, successes as well as the important people in their life before they met you. You will come to know your child much better in the process and help to build trust between you.

Some stories, however, are easier to tell than others. The more complicated your child's story, the more help you will need in coming to terms with it yourself and in dealing with your child's questions when they arrive. Never be afraid of asking your social worker for advice and help in this most difficult of areas. It will be important for you to have accepted the story and become accustomed to the emotions it will have engendered in you.

As a general rule, try to explain 'how' things happened, rather than 'why'. 'Why' carries connotations of blame, and this must be avoided wherever possible. 'How' is much less emotive and leads to a more dispassionate, realistic and practical description of events. This is not to play down the importance of the emotional aspects surrounding birth parents; they will be felt only too keenly by both you and your child.

Challenging behaviours sometimes result from your child's contemplation of their past and their biological parents. During the awkward time between childhood and adulthood, adolescents start to search for answers to questions such as 'Who am I?' 'Where do I come from?' 'Why me?' 'Why am I here?' 'Where do I belong?' 'What will I become?' It will probably be difficult to define what is causing the problem; it may just be a case of weathering the storm. Adolescents can be tricky whatever their background. Chances are you could simply be coming face to face with nature in its rawest form – that of a young teenager trying to figure themselves out and feeling in the process that the world is against them.

Use a light, easy manner when talking to your child about their past. If you have always looked through their life-story book with them and talked about the stories and the people in their life before they met you, they will appreciate this. It is important to recognise there is a right time to talk. It is wrong to make a child, or indeed anyone, talk about things they don't want to. All you can do is let them know through your actions that you are available to talk when they want and you will be honest with them. Sharing requires trust. Trust requires time and the right environment to develop; it cannot be forced.

The way your child thinks and asks questions about their adoption will change as they grow up. Beware of imposing your own views on how you would cope, or what you would want to know. Be guided by your child. Pay attention to what they say, how they say it and in what context. Listen to questions and manage them at a rate and depth dictated by your child. If you are in doubt, once again seek help early. Everyone will benefit, especially your child.

TELLING OTHERS

Telling other people about your child and the fact that they are adopted requires some thought. You must be prepared to accept that many people will know very little about what adoption involves. They may be even more ignorant of how children who have been neglected and abused can behave. So even if you mention it to someone, don't expect them to understand. This may also hold true for extended family members. From the outset it is important that you keep your intimate, close family and friends up to speed with what is happening and informed about the difficulties that may be ahead. You could, for example, share with them some of your learning from the educational aspect of your assessment. It is fair to expect this understanding and support from close family and friends who can at least 'be there' for you and listen, even though they may not be able to fix the problem.

YOUR CHILD'S BIOLOGICAL FAMILY

The older your child is when you adopt them, the more likely it is that they will already have appropriate contact with their siblings, birth families and carers. Potentially, your child comes with a collection of individuals in tow. You would be wise to find out as much as you can about them prior to adoption. You will want to consider how much contact there is and what kind of relationship would work for your family.

THE BIOLOGICAL PARENTS

The child's birth family, particularly the parent or parents, are the 'herd of elephants in the room'. What relationship do you have, or want, with your child's biological parents? This will be discussed at length during your assessment and will remain an issue for both you and your child. There is no doubt that you will have a relationship of some kind with your child's biological parents. This may be overt, where there is actual contact with them or contact through a third party. Alternatively, the relationship with them may just be in your mind, seldom spoken about and perhaps even feared.

Any parent, let alone an adoptive one, will dread the time when a child says, 'I don't love you.' The added pain for adoptive parents will come if your child says, 'You're not my real parents.' Similarly, an adopted child may dread their parents one day saying, 'I don't love you … you're not my real child.' It cuts both ways. You are the adult in the relationship and it falls to you to address this question and deal with it in an adult fashion, no matter how painful it is.

This will involve being honest with yourself and your partner about how you feel about the biological parents. This is not a matter to tuck away and ignore; you must find a way of being at peace with your feelings. Worrying about the biological parents can undermine your belief in yourself and that won't do – your child needs you to be as strong and as confident as possible. So talk about those elephants; learn how to deal with them in a way that makes you and your child comfortable. Acknowledge your fears and worries to your loved ones and social worker if necessary.

CONTACT

Without care, contact can complicate your relationship and bonding with your child. As they struggle to come to terms with what has happened to them and how they have reached this point with you, you will have to deal with any emotional fallout while endeavouring to build a new relationship with them. This is why so much time and effort is put into informing you about issues such as attachment, bonding, loss, development and trauma and how they manifest themselves in your child. The more you understand, the more able you will be to manage situations that may arise.

In some situations, contact with biological parents is detrimental to your child's physical and mental health. However, your child will come to know about their biological parents as time passes, even if they were neglectful, abusive and violent. Your child will have experienced this and it will be somewhere in their subconscious. The older the child, the longer the abuse may have been going on, and the more likely they are to have memories of it. Your child may require therapy to deal with this. Contact with other biological family members may be helpful in allowing them a greater understanding about the behaviour of one of their number.

You may prefer your child to have no contact with their biological family, particularly if your child is very young as they are likely to feel more 'yours'. Without contact, however, there may be a tendency to feel there is no need to contemplate the past. This is an unwise course of action as all adoptees will need to address their biological past at some stage. It is therefore best to normalise this from the word go rather than let them find out at a specific age, time and place; they are unlikely to thank you for this. So, even in situations of extreme abuse or neglect, allowing no contact may not be a solution.

It is important for you to consider your child's background and to come to terms with any issues that it throws up. When you are so set on starting a family it is hard to comprehend how anyone could not want their biological offspring. Harder still to grasp is the concept of mistreating them to such an extent that the authorities do not think you are fit to look after them. Inevitably, adoptive parents find it harder to cope with this type of background. People find it easier to come to terms with having a child who was voluntarily given up for adoption, although they are not the ones in the most need.

REMEMBERING AND FORGETTING: LIFE STORIES

As we pass through life we all need some fixed points in our history to hang our memories upon. Forgetting, however, is just as much a part of life as remembering. Sometimes we can forget the good things and remember only the bad. In these situations it is terribly important to try to get a more balanced view about the past and our roles in it. Sadly, it is not uncommon for children to feel responsible for any dreadful things that happened to them. They may need help to understand that this is unlikely to be the case.

Another way of coping with a disadvantaged past is to fantasise about it, to idealise it and 'carry on as normal' while knowing in your heart of hearts that something is 'not right'. Fantasy can be a way of suppressing or escaping from the past and thereby not dealing with it. It is important to be able to recognise when this is happening with your child. Empathy and sympathetic understanding of how fantasies develop will help you to be perceptive, gentle and patient in aiding your child to accept and acknowledge difficult truths from their past. Empathy is at the core of good parenting. When your child feels wanted, loved, respected and valued they will come to feel safe and able to risk trusting you; they may even be able to relinquish some of their fantasies.

Few of us can remember a great deal about our early childhoods. If we're not adopted we have the benefit of being able to explore the past by asking members of our biological family for information on our family history; we are likely also to have family heirlooms to rummage through. Seeking information about the past is both human and natural, and as we get older we tend to become more interested in it. Like you, your child will want to do the same at some stage. It is your duty, and hopefully your desire, to help them. This will be made easier for you if you have been given your child's life-story book.

THE LIFE-STORY BOOK

The life-story book is prepared by your child's social worker and those who have cared for your child before they come to you; you will naturally add to this record. Your child's social worker will also provide them with what is known as a later-life letter. This is a letter to your child written in age-appropriate language explaining how they came to be placed for adoption. The life-story book aims to fill in the gaps for your child about their life before they came to join your family. It is perhaps best described as a pictorial history book on the life of your child. Although it is given to you at a designated time after placement, the life-story book belongs to your child. It is a record of fundamental importance to both of you.

The life-story book should contain details of:

➤ when and how your child came to be adopted
➤ their birth parents and other members of their biological family
➤ where they were cared for and by whom
➤ important events, anniversaries and experiences

There should also be photographs, letters and drawings. This record is to help your child come to understand more about themselves. It is also a powerful tool for your child to share with you, and to help you get to know each other better.

If no life-story book exists then you can create one with your child. This can be a most positive and productive experience. It gives you the chance to work together to seek information about the practical details of your child's route to adoption and about their heritage and cultural background. You are likely to learn at least as much as your child in this venture.

Life-story work can also be emotional and difficult for both you and your child. You may have to deal with all sorts of emotions that come up as you work together on the project. As this work is so important for your child, you will want to go through this with them, no matter how difficult a ride it may be. You will have to deal not only with your own emotional reactions but also those of your child. In such an emotional area, shared experiences and stress can actually bring you together. It is a wonderful opportunity for you to show your child, through your actions, that you are able to cope with difficult, and possibly unpleasant, information and yet still be strong and there for them. This will not only help your child develop the necessary skills to deal with the problems in the past, but will also show them a way of coping in the present and thereby the future.

At these times you will need support from your partner, family and social groups in order to stay strong for your child. When the going gets tough it may also help to remember that you are investing in your child's future and helping them to lay firm foundations in their character. They will be learning not to be afraid of the past, to face it with courage and resilience and make peace with it.

Sometimes, however, information from your child's past may be particularly difficult or distasteful. In these situations it is essential for you to seek professional advice on how to manage this with your child. Confusion and fantasy may fill the vacuum created by lack of information, but eventually reality will intrude, the truth will out, and you will need to plan how to manage the situation in an honest and age-sensitive way. If the child has been damaged by particularly distasteful experiences and this is recognised before placement, details of any psychotherapy required will be part and parcel of their Adoption

Placement Plan. You will need to know how best to support them during this.

Your child's past is an unavoidable part of your future together. Helping them to value their past is crucial to your child's sense of identity and will deepen your knowledge and awareness of who they are. While it is not always easy to talk about some aspects of their history, working together on their life story will be an emotional experience for you and your child, and may help deepen your relationship.

CHAPTER 12

Getting Ongoing Help and Support

Parenting a child is a huge emotional enterprise, throughout which the focus has been squarely on your child. In all this upheaval you may have forgotten about yourself. You must remember that you are truly vital to the whole process. It is therefore important that you look after yourself.

Once you have adopted your child and are getting on with day-to-day parenting, there is still support available for you and your child, should you need it. In this chapter we will look at the types of support you can access, ranging from post-adoption services to health care and training. We will also look at what to do in the unlikely event of serious problems occurring in the adoption.

ADOPTION SUPPORT SERVICES

Although the granting of an Adoption Order is a triumph for everyone involved, the job is far from done. These days, there is much more emphasis on supporting parents after the adoption than there was in the past. Post-adoption support is based upon an evaluation of your needs before the placement is made. This judgement will be made using information gleaned during the assessment process for both you and your child.

Before you start to beat yourself up for poor parenting when you run into a problem, remember that it is likely to have something to do with issues in your child's past. It could be a matter that was raised in the early days of the adoption process that you might have forgotten about. Dig out the relevant files and notes, reread them and see if there are any clues. It may be you have to think again about what help and support you are getting. You are entitled to ask for a reassessment if you feel that would help.

Needs may be general or particular. Most new parents require reassurance; as adoptive parents, you will be no different. You will want to know that everything is going okay and that you're doing the right things. It helps to have people with whom to compare notes, and this is where your social network comes in. You will probably talk to family and friends first, but if you are fortunate you will also have a new and highly valuable resource at your disposal: your fellow adopters. During the assessment process, you may have got to know other people going through adoption. Their experiences give them an 'expertise' which can be extremely helpful. There is nothing more reassuring than talking to someone in the same boat, knowing you are not alone. Just as pregnant women keep in touch after their babies are born, it is excellent if you can do that with other adoptive parents. As a peer support charity for adoptive parents, Adoption UK offers a range of parent-to-parent services that connect parents who have pressing questions about adoption with people who have answers based on their own experience. This includes the Parents Are Liked (PAL) database, a range of contact networks and support groups, and numerous online message boards (see Resources, page 248).

As a parent it's not easy or pleasant to face the fact that you may occasionally have failed in a certain department or that you are handling a particular problem badly. It is even harder to hear that from others. This is where you have to thicken your skin. People usually mean well when they chip in with advice, although it can be incredibly irritating if it is unasked for and unwanted. Depending on your relationship with your family members and friends, it will be important to try and see comments in a positive light and not as a criticism of your parenting ability or your child. Then again, if you can't achieve that degree of equanimity it might be best to avoid a confrontation in the first place. Avoid the subject when you are with them or tell them outright that you do not want them to be involved. You want support, not unhelpful meddling.

There are times when you will be only too aware that help is needed. Sometimes, however, other people will notice first. Members of your family or friends, and perhaps even your GP or social worker, may pick up clues that things are not quite right. Your child may be seen to have difficulties making relationships, not only within the family but also at school with their peer group. It may be that teachers have concerns about your child's behaviour or progress.

An even harder pill to swallow is if other parents are commenting on possible problems, spotting that something is wrong before you do. In this instance you have to take a deep breath, swallow your pride with the pill and treat the situation as an attempt to help rather than hinder. You cannot be with your child 24/7 and kids will say all sorts of things when out of your hearing; they are masters of nonsense and imagination. Another parent should appreciate this but it could be that their antennae are tuned in to spot troubles because your child has been adopted. The actions of the other parent are unlikely to be malevolent; they probably just want to help. Treat what they tell you as information you can use for the good of your child, like having another pair of eyes and ears.

It takes a great deal of maturity to accept such advice, particularly if you feel unsure about your parenting skills. Recognising that you need help is not a sign of weakness; this cannot be stressed strongly or often enough. Acknowledging there is a problem, trying to solve it with the strategies you have and, where necessary, seeking advice, information and help makes you a fine role model, not only for parenting but also for your children.

TRAINING

You are likely to be offered training by your adoption agency. It would be worth attending any training sessions offered, particularly on topics such as separation and loss, abuse, neglect and trauma. If your child is unfortunate enough to require therapy for any of these experiences then you will need to request further help and advice. Talk to your social worker, GP and those in the child and adolescent mental health services about how you can best help your child through the therapeutic process. Find out, too, what steps you can take to look after your own mental health so you can support your child without damaging yourself or any other family members in the process.

LOOKING AFTER YOUR HEALTH

Your child will arrive with a ready-made repertoire of behaviours. If this is your first child you'll be right in at the deep end. Your child may be settled, confident and emotionally available from the outset. They may be quiet and withdrawn or bouncing off the walls. Whatever their behaviour, you can be sure that you will react to it emotionally with feelings ranging from excitement, anticipation and enjoyment through worry and apprehension to irritation and even anger. Just like a roller-coaster ride, you are likely to feel excited at times and scared at others. You can't get off even if you want to, but at the end you will look back on it with a sense of achievement.

Placement and adoption of your child is a major life event for you, your child and your family. It is not an emotionally neutral event and involves loss and gain. The most obvious loss will be that of tranquillity. Emotional richness is the most noticeable gain. As with any emotional trial, it is important to get the support of those who are important to you; they need not do very much apart from be with you on this part of your journey.

DEALING WITH THE BLUES AND DEPRESSION

In both childbirth and adoption, positive and negative emotional experiences are common. The focus is naturally upon the positive aspects but it is important to recognise lowered mood when it occurs as this may blend imperceptibly into full-blown depression in both situations. The psychiatric conditions following childbirth are very serious and are thought to be related to an interaction between genetic susceptibility and the hormonal changes involved in pregnancy. Adoptive mothers will clearly not be affected by hormonal triggers; therefore any lowering of mood is likely to be related to clear external environmental triggers. Fortunately, once these triggers are identified they can usually be rectified.

The adoption process is physically and emotionally demanding. It is important to look after yourself at every stage along the way. You are likely to get occasional periods of the so-called post-adoption 'blues' when you feel low, tearful and emotional. These are the blues rather than depression because they don't last very long and relate clearly to specific episodes or periods of exhaustion. After all the excitement and effort of the assessment, matching and placement, the blues are a normal reaction to the awareness of the enormity of the task you've taken on and the responsibility involved. Low periods are particularly likely to happen when you're exhausted. It is therefore important to get as much rest as possible as most people's ability to cope with stress is diminished when they're tired.

Depression, on the other hand, is important to recognise as it can interfere with your relationship with your child and other important people. It is a lowering of mood that doesn't lift and has the following characteristics:

➤ You lose your drives and energy for life.
➤ Things become difficult, an effort, and life's little problems can seem insurmountable.
➤ It becomes difficult to make decisions and the future seems less clear.

➤ Sleep doesn't make you feel refreshed.

➤ Food is less appealing.

➤ Irritability is common.

➤ You think it's your fault, and that if only you could 'snap out of it' everything would be okay.

➤ You look on the bleak side of everything.

➤ You may even come to loathe yourself.

Depression affects the way you feel and think about yourself and can add to any negative feelings you may have about your parenting skills, thereby compounding your misery. It is common to hear comments such as, 'I've worked so hard to have this child, I am so lucky, I should not be feeling like . . .' These sentiments only serve to add to distress. These feelings are real; accept them and seek help.

The symptoms of depression frequently start insidiously and can be quite subtle and difficult to spot in their early stages. So, if you don't feel right, talk to someone early because depression will interfere with your life and your ability to look after your child. That's the bad news. The good news is that it's treatable, particularly if caught early. You are more likely to make a good recovery if attention is paid not only to the psychological and physical aspects of your condition, but also to your needs for advice and support in looking after your child.

Remember: you are not alone and you are not weak. Whatever you do, go easy on yourself. Allow yourself to make mistakes. You are only human, not super-human, no matter how much you might wish you were.

TAKE TIME FOR YOURSELF

It is easy in all this emotional upheaval to forget one of the key players – you. It won't be a deliberate oversight; just a symptom of the situation you are in. You will be putting other people's needs before your own, which is quite natural. However, as much as you have to invest in loved ones, you must also look after yourself. Without you the whole adoption train will be derailed. See yourself and your wellbeing as a vital resource that must be nurtured and cared for.

One of the greatest gifts we can give anyone is time, so give some to yourself. As a parent you will need to restore your energy and enthusiasm so you can reinvest them in your new family to everyone's benefit. You should give yourself boundaries, just as you do with your child. It is impossible, and undesirable, to be there for everyone 100 per cent of the time and give 150 per cent of your effort every day. It will set a dangerous precedent; you will become exhausted and it may be difficult to change this habit later on.

You may be one of those people who is able to ring-fence a slice of the day for themselves. Then again, if you are like most of us you will have thought about it but never quite got around to doing it. Now is the occasion to master the art. It isn't too difficult to establish a routine; the trouble is following it. Once you have designated a block of time for yourself, let everyone know this is what you are doing and that you are not to be bothered. Take yourself away to your own room or study; turn off the phones and do not answer the door. Have a nap if you can; read a book; distract yourself; try not to think about the matters that are worrying you. Switch off completely. It may be that all you need to do is go for a good walk – take the dog if you have one and do two jobs at once.

Your child may not understand your actions. Therefore it is essential that you make clear, from the outset, that your stepping back from the world for a short time does not mean you are rejecting them. It may take your child a while to develop this understanding. Their experience may have been that withdrawal and silence were tools of anger. You must be able to reassure them that this is not the case. The most powerful way to do this is by modelling (see page 196) – not only using good words but backing them up with clear action too. Children are used to grasping routines; they like them as they help them know where they stand. So if you disappear at a certain time each day, or in the evening, it will be something they come to expect. If they are old enough, explain what you are doing.

You are not the only one who warrants this kind of special consideration. You should ensure that everyone in the family has as much protected time set aside as they need. Managing your child's need for protected time depends on their age. It is important to respect their wishes. Establishing this part of the new regime will require trust and understanding on your part. It might be difficult at first but the situation will improve as your relationship develops.

ALWAYS SEEK HELP EARLY

We all look to the future, especially when it comes to our children. We plot and plan for the best-case scenario. Have you heard the joke: 'How do you make God laugh? Show him your plans'? I think that just about sums up how life can be. You can prepare yourself and others as much as possible; you may be bursting with knowledge, competence and confidence but the reality is that things do not always work out how you expect them to. When things go wrong in adoption there is a huge amount at risk, so keeping a careful eye on troubles is crucial.

The assessment cannot foresee some of the difficulties you may encounter. Serious problems can develop that tear through the life you have built together, such as the death of a blood or adoptive relative, financial or health crises or emotional instability. When this happens you cannot afford to sit back and wait to see how things pan out. It is a time for action, to 'seek help early'. Every professional will tell you the same thing. You have to act quickly before things get out of hand and put the adoption, your health, the health of your family and, of course, the health and security of your child at risk.

In essence, the more support available the less likely it is that the adoption will fail. The earlier you raise the alarm the better chance you have of holding things together. The support is there but it is useless unless you make the decision to ask for it, so if things are looking bleak right now, pick up the phone.

DISRUPTION

It is impossible to be prepared for every eventuality involved in adoption. Perhaps the most distressing for all parties is when a placement or adoption fails. This is termed 'disruption'. A collapse of this severity is the exception; definitely not the rule. Given the extreme complexity of the task in matching and placing children with adoptive parents, it is perhaps a testament to the effectiveness of the assessment procedure that so many adoptions prove successful.

The rates of disruption are between 10 and 20 per cent. These figures can appear quite high until you look at it the other way round, namely that 80–90 per cent of adoptions and placements work out. Disruptions are more likely to occur as children get older, particularly around the time of adolescence. However, this does not mean that all placements in this age group fail; far from it.

Every case has unique factors at play. When disruption happens it is, of course, a serious business for all parties. The damage goes beyond you and the child, affecting family, friends and agency workers involved. When disruption does occur, a lot of effort is put into exploring the reasons for this, and these studies have helped to mould current adoption practice.

Certain risk factors make disruption more probable. These may reside in the child, the adoptive parents or the adoption agency. In most cases they interact in a complicated way and without careful handling they can lead adoptive parents to prematurely withdraw from the process before exploring, and exhausting, all avenues of help and support. Throughout this book I have stressed the importance of seeking help early to try to prevent failure of the adoptive process which harms all parties involved. Disruption is more likely if seeking help is delayed.

YOUR CHILD AND DISRUPTION

Disruption may occur if your child has emotional and behavioural difficulties. A major risk factor is if there has been an inadequate assessment of your child's health, emotional and social development and needs. Another danger is a lack of preparation for placement with you. Also, distress felt by the child at separation from earlier important carers, family and friends in their life can increase the risk of a breakdown.

It will be important for your child to have had some psychotherapeutic preparation, support and possibly counselling before and after placement with you. They should have a good relationship with their social worker, and their current carers should be in a position to be able to 'let go' of your child in a positive way. Their placement with you should not be too hasty, and any specialist resources required should be available when needed. If your child has a history of being abused, a large number of moves in care or a disruption of a previous adoptive placement, they may have more difficulty in developing emotional attachment with you and other members of your family. This may be exacerbated if there are any continuing problematic relationships with other members of their birth family.

If matters are really bad it could mean your child's behaviours will be so extreme, unacceptable and possibly dangerous that separation is the only option for everyone's physical safety and mental health. It is terribly sad, frustrating, distressing and undermining to feel things went wrong despite so much effort on everyone's part. Sometimes children just decide they don't want to be part of your family any more and there is little you can do to change their mind. Sometimes behaviours that were deeply buried come to the surface. You will want to understand how disruption could happen, especially if you are planning to give adoption another go.

YOU AND DISRUPTION

Certain factors make disruption more probable. For instance, it is more likely if placement coincides with other major life changes. Simple things like having to travel long distances for introductions over an extended period of time can also take their toll. Your child's behaviour may disturb the equilibrium, and occasionally health, of other members of the family in a way that is difficult to resolve. With the best will in the world, and after all the in-depth preparation you've been through, disruption is more likely if you don't have a clear understanding of your child's development and background, and if your expectations of your child differ greatly from the reality. Without appropriate help, advice and support, disruption may occur. It is essential that your assessment has empowered you not only to embrace your child and their difficulties but also to understand the need to seek professional advice earlier rather than later, before problems become more difficult to manage.

You are likely to have a deep desire for a family and the compassion, commitment and determination to hang on in there, come hell or high water, hoping things will improve. Sometimes your expectations will not be matched by the reality of your parenting experience. For a placement to be successful, your understanding of parenting needs to move smoothly from the intellectual to the practical. What you need to do is care for and manage your child on a daily basis. You may feel simply burnt out by the experience, or that you have not been heard or supported with your difficulties and concerns.

Sometimes, despite six to eight months of intensive thought, study and assessment, it is only when you meet your child for the first time that you are able to identify how you feel about becoming a prospective parent. Although withdrawing at this stage is distressing, it is better than commencing a placement having serious doubts nagging at the back of your mind.

THE ADOPTION AGENCY AND DISRUPTION

Disruption is more likely if the local authority has failed to put in place the necessary and appropriate support. There is no excuse for an inadequate assessment of your child's needs. All the information the adoption agency has on the child should be made available to you. A failure in the gathering of information or passing it on to you, for whatever reason, may also increase the risk of disruption. However, sometimes the child's problems will not become clear until after they have been placed with you. Therefore it is essential to maintain your contact with your local authority as they are legally required to reassess your needs, particularly if circumstances change. It is also important that the adoption agency pays great attention to the process of initial introductions; if mishandled, these may sow the seeds for disruption. Occasionally, there may be unforeseen events that interfere with the placement process, such as a change of social worker at a crucial time.

PREVENTING DISRUPTION

No one wants to fail, especially when dealing with the lives of others. The possibility of disruption may sit inside your head, nagging away at you in the background. While acknowledging the possibility of disruption, it is important to focus on the positive aspects of the adoption process. Squash that nasty little voice; the last thing you want to do is create a self-fulfilling prophecy. It may also be something your child picks up on, detecting your fears through your reactions and behaviours. Chances are they will proceed to mirror those fears and start a downward spiral.

Your words must match your actions and non-verbal communications. These should all give the very clear message that you have the desire, ability, commitment and stamina to make the placement work. When the going gets tough, draw on your reserves and resiliencies to prove to your child that all will be well. There can be nothing more distressing than a disruption if you cannot honestly put your hand on your heart and say you did everything you could to make it work. Despite the challenges and any doubts you may have it is worth remembering that you have probably been doing a better job than many birth parents would in similar circumstances. You will have had more training and preparation for the role and more outside support.

As adopting parents, you will want to know that your child's needs have been fully assessed and, where appropriate, addressed before you contemplate a placement. Part of this assessment must include a discussion as to what help and support your child, you and your family will require before, during and after placement in order to give it the best chance of success. Your child's requirements for support will change with time. Indeed, it often calls for security and time before a child's real needs become clear. You have a key role in the process of providing the professionals with the information they require to help. You are the advocate for your child; it is your job to champion their cause.

Most professionals who work with children are committed and driven by a desire to improve the quality of life for them. If, however, you are unfortunate enough to run into difficulties with professionals it is important to have a full and frank discussion from the outset. Like the rest of us, adoption agency staff do not always get it right; hopefully, you will have a good enough relationship with them to accept this. Slipshod, incompetent or unprofessional behaviour is, however, utterly unacceptable at any stage. Should you feel this to be the case, complain. You could talk to others who are adopting or who have already been through the process to see if the problems you are encountering are unusual enough for you to be concerned.

Disruption may be preventable if you seek help early. Your local authority should not make you feel as if you are being judged or blamed if things are going wrong. You should feel that seeking help is a normal thing for you to do. Adoption requires a lot of effort by everyone involved. Exhaustion is a potent demoraliser and when things are particularly fraught, everybody will benefit from a break, a respite, from the problem and each other: a chance to recharge batteries, to rest and take time to reflect on what has happened; a time to seek help and advice from friends, family, your social worker, and perhaps even your GP. Rest can lead to a renewed desire and determination to find solutions. Respite can range from a weekend to a week or two away from each other, getting other family members to look after your child while you go away or simply stay at home peacefully. Seek help sooner rather than later and discuss your needs with family and friends as well as other adoptive parents and professionals.

DISRUPTION MEETING

After such a long and arduous journey involving a great many people and an enormous investment of time and effort, disruption is understandably distressing and potentially damaging for everyone. In the unlikely event of it happening, the local authority convenes what is called a disruption meeting.

The impetus of a disruption meeting is to identify how the placement broke down. It also aims to discover how your child, you, your family and the adoption agency can obtain understanding, some 'closure' and healing. The desire is for not only you but also your child to move on, to reinvest in the future and try again. After the meeting a report will be compiled and circulated for comments and feedback before a final report is made available to all relevant parties.

The meeting will examine how the events unfolded over time as well as information available to adoption agencies prior to the placement. It will look at:

➤ form (E), which includes a profile of your child
➤ your child's care plan and assessment
➤ the proposed placement plan

➤ the post-adoption support plan
➤ the matching form and minutes of the adoption
   panel's deliberations in your case as well as the
   record of the legally required reviews

You, and perhaps other members of your family, will be invited, as will your child, where appropriate. Both your and your child's social workers and other support workers will be invited, as will the manager of the adoption agency and other agencies involved, such as health services, mental health services and teachers. It may also be thought appropriate to include members of your child's birth family. You may wish to seek legal advice if you feel that the proper procedures were not followed during your assessment, the assessment of the child, the matching and placement, particularly if you think information has been withheld.

Most adoption placements are successful. While this chapter has given you information on what to do if the worst happens, I hope the more general advice on seeking help and advice is something you will take on board. Prevention is better than cure so it is best to seek help as soon as you feel it is needed.

What Now?

It is impossible to be prepared for every eventuality involved in adoption. Whatever hurdles you encounter, seek information. The aim of post-placement and post-adoption support is to augment your natural coping mechanisms and informal support network such as family and friends. By staying focused on the present and dealing with problems as they come up, you will be able to create a firm foundation for your and your child's future.

PLANNING YOUR FUTURE TOGETHER

Both you and your child will naturally be apprehensive about the future, given the trials and tribulations you have both endured to get to this point. It is therefore important to discuss and plan for the future. It gives a clear message to your child that they are part of something that will endure over time. Your child may have developed a strategy of coping by living from day to day. They may shrink from thinking about the future as they probably felt they had little control over it.

While it is healthy to plan for the future, it is important to make sure you are living in the present. The future is an abstract concept; too much emphasis on it, or indeed on the past, can diminish the energy available to live in the present to the best effect. Putting effort into the here and now is never wasted. You can profitably spend time just 'being with' each other, learning about one another and consolidating your relationship. Paying attention to the present lays the foundations of a more solid future.

There is the possibility that you will want to adopt another child. If things have gone as well as they should then you are in an excellent position to go through the process again when the time is right for you all.

CELEBRATING SUCCESSES

It is only natural to highlight difficulties, as this is where solutions are required. However, it's important to acknowledge successes on a daily basis. Problems are less frequent than books will have you believe – in much the same way that news items are nearly always stories about unusual events. The statistics indicate that the extreme problems mentioned in Chapter 12 are uncommon. Chances are that your son or daughter has adapted well to their new family, and that you have achieved your goal of becoming a parent. It is a wonderful feeling. Take time to savour it and to share your success with those who have helped you.

GETTING ON WITH PARENTING

Once you have got to this stage you may decide you have had quite enough to do with bureaucracy. You will probably be sick to death of filling in forms, answering personal questions and generally allowing strangers into your life to sit in judgement. You may want to avoid adoption agencies like the plague. Finally, after all the months and years of scrutiny, you may feel an overwhelming desire to just 'get on' with being a parent, secure in your new-found family. And who can blame you? It will not have been an easy journey but hopefully you feel it is more than worthwhile when you see first hand how you have changed the life of another person. In all probability you will need little input from the professionals and will be able to manage all of the special issues relating to your child without external assistance.

GIVING SOMETHING BACK

This desire to detach yourself may be permanent or it could be something that wears off as you become more confident in your parenting role. You do not have to keep in touch with the adoption services for a negative reason. It could be that once the dust has settled you will want to put something back. You are now not only a parent but an expert on adoption. Whether your experiences have been good or bad you may want to help others negotiate difficult situations with the benefit of your hindsight. This is always warmly welcomed by those starting out on the process, as well as those in the thick of it. If you cast your mind back you will be able to see at which stages you would have most welcomed hearing from someone like yourself. You will know that sharing your experiences and realising that you are not alone can provide a powerful boost in times of difficulties. You can offer another family these benefits at no cost to yourself other than a bit of time.

You may be in a position to advocate more generally on behalf of adoption and children in search of families; for example getting involved in media events, writing books and fundraising. Whatever you do, you will be most welcome. Rest assured that your contribution, however small, will make a difference – sometimes an exceptionally important one – in the lives of an adopting family and an adopted child. So, if you feel inclined, just do it. You won't regret it.

If you've read this far you've clearly got the 'right stuff'. With the help of this and other books, you'll know where to start and what to expect. Adoption is a wonderful human act of conscious love. If you think you can, you can. Good luck.

References

INTRODUCTION

1 http://www.statistics.gov.uk/cci/nugget.asp?id=592
2 http://www.dfes.gov.uk/rsgateway/DB/SFR/s000741/ index. shtml

CHAPTER 1

3 This refers to all adoption orders granted (for example, including step parent adoption) and not simply adoptions from the care system, which this book is focused on.
4 http://www.baaf.org.uk/info/firstq/adoption.shtml

CHAPTER 2

5 Jenny C, Roesler TA, Poyer KL, 1994, 'Are children at risk for sexual abuse by homosexuals?', *Paediatrics*, 94 (1), pp 41–4
6 Allen M and Burrell N, 1996, 'Comparing the impact of homosexual and heterosexual parents on children: meta-analysis of existing research', *Journal of Homosexuality*, 32, pp19–35
7 http://www.opsi.gov.uk/si/si2003/20031173.htm
8 Statutory Instrument 2005 No. 1109 The Special Guardianship Regulations 2005 online at http://www.opsi.gov.uk/si/si2005/20051109.htm

CHAPTER 4

9 http://www.lv.com/media_centre/press_releases/cost

Resources

This book is a starter in your quest for knowledge about adoption. There are a large number of publications, perhaps too many to read for any one human. I have therefore kept this section very brief as a little goes a long way. It is impossible to proceed without acknowledging the pre-eminence of the British Association of Adoption and Fostering (BAAF) and Adoption UK in this field.

USEFUL ORGANISATIONS

Adoption UK

www.adoptionuk.org
Adoption UK exists 'to provide support, friendship and information to adopters and prospective adopters'.

The BBC

www.bbc.co.uk

Be My Parent

www.bemyparent.org.uk
Be My Parent is a UK-wide family-finding service provided by the British Association for Adoption and Fostering (BAAF).

British Association of Adoption and Fostering (BAAF)

www.baaf.org.uk
BAAF's website is a veritable Tardis of information and I would recommend you go there first.

Channel 4

www.channel4.com

The BBC and Channel 4 websites have excellent sections on
adoption and parenting, some of which stems from their
programme output. Both of these sites will direct you to BAAF
and Adoption UK.

Children Who Wait

www.adoptionuk.org

When you become a member of Children Who Wait you will be
able to access the family-finding service of the charity Adoption
UK either online or through the magazine.

Directgov

www.direct.gov.uk

The official government website for UK citizens and has excellent
links.

National Association for the Care and Resettlement of Offenders (NACRO)

0800 0181 259

helpline@nacro.org.uk

Office of Public Sector Information

www.opsi.gov.uk

You can obtain details of all the necessary UK legislation from this site.

Post-adoption Centre

5 Torriano Mews, Torriano Road, London NW5 2RZ
020 7284 5879
www.postadoptioncentre.org.uk

Stonewall

Tower Building, York Road, London SE1 7NX
08000 50 20 20 (Mon–Fri 9.30am to 5.30pm)
www.stonewall.org.uk

FURTHER READING

If you are more at home with books, I would recommend starting with the following BAAF publications which are regularly updated:

Adopting a child. A guide for people interested in adoption by Jenifer Lord, 2008. (IBSN 978-1-905664-56-5)

This is an engaging and easy read that will provide you with a list of all the adoption agencies in the country as well as other useful information when starting out.

The Adopters' Handbook. Information, resources and services for adoptive parents by Amy Neil Salter, 2006. (IBSN 1-903699-92-4)

This is a mine of information and an absolute must for anyone considering adoption. The author lists over 100 books for prospective adopters, adoptive parents and adopted or fostered children, as well as details of journals, magazines and publishers in this area. Organisations, government agencies and websites are also included, covering everything from adoption support agencies and research institutes to charities.

Bibliography

BOOKS AND PAPERS

Adopters on adoption. Reflections on parenthood and children, David Howe, BAAF 1996

Adopting a child. A guide for people interested in adoption, Jenifer Lord, BAAF 2008

Adoption Undone. A painful story of an adoption breakdown, Karen Carr, BAAF 2007

An Adoption Diary. A couple's journey from infertility to parenthood, Maria James, BAAF 2006

Considering Adoption?, Sarah Biggs, Sheldon Press 2000

John Bowlby & Attachment Theory, Jeremy Holmes, Routledge 1993

Keys to Solution in Brief Therapy, Steve de Shazer, WW Norton and Company 1985

'Lesbian and gay parenting: babes in arms or babes in the woods?', D McCann and H Delmonte, *Sexual & Relationship Therapy*, Volume 20, Number 3, August 2005, pp 333–347(15)

Loving and living with traumatised children, Reflections by adoptive parents, Megan Hirst, BAAF 2005

'Outcome of adoption from public care: research and practice issues', A Rushton, *Advances in Psychiatric Treatment*, Volume 13, 2007, pp 305–311

Preparing for Permanence (Booklet). *Key Issues in Assessment. Points to address during the assessment process*, BAAF 1998

Preparing for Permanence (Booklet). *Assessment. Points to consider for those assessing potential adopters and foster carers*, BAAF 1998

Preparing for Permanence (Booklet). *Understanding the assessment process. Information for prospective adopters and foster carers*, BAAF 1998

Recruiting, assessing and supporting lesbian and gay carers and adopters, GP Mallon and B Betts, BAAF 2005

The Adopters' Handbook. Information, resources and services for adoptive parents, Amy Neil Salter, BAAF 2006

The Adoption Experience. Families who give children a second chance, Ann Morris, Jessica Kingsley Publishers 1999

The adoption process in England. A guide for children's social workers, Jenifer Lord, BAAF 2008

The Post-Adoption Blues. Overcoming the unforeseen challenges of adoption, KJ Foli and JR Thompson, Rodale Publishers 2004

The Primal Wound. Understanding the Adopted Child, Nancy Newton Verrier, Gateway Press 1991

Understanding Attachment and Attachment Disorders. Theory, Evidence and Practice, V Prior and D Glaser, Jessica Kingsley Publishers 2006

Online Material

A study of childlessness in Britain, The Joseph Rowntree Foundation, July 1998, Ref. 738 http://www.jrf.org.uk/

About Adoption from the Be My Parent website (Be My Parent is a UK-wide family-finding service provided by the British Association for Adoption and Fostering), http://www.bemyparent.org.uk/info-for-families/about-adoption/

Adoptees and relatives who wish to contact one another: the Adoption Contact Register. J Haskey and R Errington, *Population Trends*, 2001, no. 104, p 18

Adoption Interlink UK, www.billsimpson.com/menu.html

Adoption Legislation, www.opsi.gov.uk/index.htm

Adoption Line UK, www.adoption.org.uk/information/default.html

Adoption Placement Report (Form F). Available as a pdf file from www.baaf.org.uk

Adoption training materials. A learning package to support the implementation of the Adoption and Children Act 2002, www.everychildmatters.gov.uk/socialcare/childrenin care/adoption/materials/

Awakenings. Simple Solutions for Life, www.lessonsforliving.com/
Barnsley Metropolitan Borough Council website,
    www.barnsley.gov.uk/bguk
BBC Parenting links, www.bbc.co.uk/parenting
Belfast Health and Social Care Trust website,
    www.belfasttrust.hscni.net/seb%20services/adoption.html
Changing Minds, www.changingminds.org/
Channel 4 parenting site,
    www.channel4.com/health/microsites/F/family/parenting/
Child development stages,
    http://en.wikipedia.org/wiki/Child_development_stages
Children looked after in England (including adoption and care
    leavers) year ending 31 March 2007. Department of Children
    Schools and Families,
    www.dcsf.gov.uk/rsgateway/DB/SFR/s000741/index.shtml
Citizens Advice Bureau, www.adviceguide.org.uk
Developmental Psychology – children,
    www.encarta.msn.com/encnet/refpages/RefEdList.aspx?refid=21
    0054891
Developmental Psychology (@ Psychology Wicki),
    www.psychology.wikia.com/wiki/Category:Developmental_psyc
    hology
East Lothian Council website, www.eastlothian.gov.uk/content/
Every Parent Matters,
    www.direct.gov.uk/en/Nl1/Newsroom/DG_066880
Family Futures Consortium, www.familyfutures.co.uk
Herefordshire Council, www.herefordshire.gov.uk/
    health/social_services/adoption.aspx
Herefordshire Council, Child's Adoption Case Records,
    www.herefordshire.gov.uk/adoption_procedures/chapters/p_ado
    p_caserec.html
Independent Review Mechanism, www.irm-adoption.org.uk/
Islington Council website,
    www.islington.gov.uk/Health/ChildAndFamilyServices/Adoption
    AndFostering
Leicester City Council website, www.leicester.gov.uk/health-social-
    care.asp

Outcome indicators for looked after children: twelve months to 30 December 2004, England (2005), www.dcsf.gov.uk/rsgateway/DB/SFR/s000727/ maincommentary.pdf

Permanence Planning: Notes for Practitioners, Adoption and Permanence Taskforce, (2004) Social Care Institute for Excellence, London, www.scie-socialcareonline.org.uk/repository/ adoption/index.asp

Plymouth City Council website, www.plymouth.gov.uk/homepage.htm

Practice Guidance on Assessing the Support Needs of Adoptive Families, www.everychildmatters.gov.uk/resources-and-practice/ig00028/

Surrey County Council website, www.surreycc.gov.uk

The Proportion of Adoptees Who Have Received Their Birth Records in England and Wales, Methods used to create adoptee estimates, R Rushbrooke, 2001, Population Trends, no 104, p 9, www.statistics.gov.uk/cci/article.asp?ID=589

Your Child's Mental Health, www.direct.gov.uk/en/Parents/Yourchildshealthandsafety/YourC hildsHealth/DG_10026100

Index